Southern Living GARDEN GUIDE
Container Gardening

Series Editor: *Lois Trigg Chaplin*

Text by *Jennifer Greer*

Oxmoor House®

©1999 by Oxmoor House, Inc.
Book Division of Southern Progress Corporation
P.O. Box 2463, Birmingham, Alabama 35201

Southern Living® is a federally registered
trademark of Southern Living, Inc.

Library of Congress Catalog Number: 96-71090
ISBN: 0-8487-2252-3
Manufactured in the United States of America
First Printing 1999

Editor-in-Chief: Nancy Fitzpatrick Wyatt
Editorial Director, Special Interest Publications:
Ann H. Harvey
Senior Editor, Editorial Services: Olivia Kindig Wells
Art Director: James Boone

Southern Living Garden Guide
CONTAINER GARDENING

Series Editor: Lois Trigg Chaplin
Assistant Editor: Kelly Hooper Troiano
Copy Editor: L. Amanda Owens
Editorial Assistant: Lauren Caswell Brooks
Garden Editor, *Southern Living*: Linda C. Askey
Indexer: Katharine R. Wiencke
Designer: Carol Loria
Senior Photographer, *Southern Living*: Van Chaplin
Director, Production and Distribution: Phillip Lee
Associate Production Manager: Vanessa C. Richardson

Our appreciation to the staff of *Southern Living*
magazine for their contributions to this book.

Special Thanks
Jim Bathie (photographs,
51 bottom, 56, 72 bottom)
Charlotte Hagood
Jennifer Sharpton
Sandra Smith
Leslie Wells

Cover: *Geraniums*
Frontispiece: (*Front to back*) *Rex begonia
and purple heart; lavender, red, and pink
chrysanthemums; dragon tree*

Geraniums and Swedish ivy

We're here for you!

We at Oxmoor House are dedicated to serving you with reliable information
that expands your imagination and enriches your life. We welcome
your comments and suggestions. Please write us at:

Oxmoor House, Inc.
Editor, Garden Guide CONTAINER GARDENING
2100 Lakeshore Drive
Birmingham, AL 35209

Contents

Daffodils, hyacinths, and pansies

Blue juniper and pansies

Container Gardening Primer

For centuries, container gardening has been a testimony to the gardener's resourcefulness, eye for beauty, and love of plants.

No matter where they lived, gardeners have always grown favorite plants in pots—on balconies, on lawns of estates, on porches of farmhouses, on rooftops of skyscrapers, in courtyards, on apartment window ledges, and even on the decks of houseboats. Once you experience the difference that containers make in your garden, you may find yourself harvesting lemon herbs or cutting roses for a bouquet—all from plants in pots.

You will discover many good reasons to garden in containers. Fill pots with plants to create a minigarden or to enhance a large garden. Replant containers seasonally to quickly and inexpensively update the garden and to ensure that something is always in bloom. Keep evergreens in containers by your doorway year-round or grow temperamental or tender plants, such as citrus trees or lavender, in containers so that you have more control over their environment. To attract butterflies, bees, and hummingbirds, select such plants as lantana, salvia, or sedum for containers on your deck or patio.

This mounted planter filled with pink impatiens extends a gracious invitation to visitors.

Container gardens require no digging, weeding, mowing, or raking. The most important activity involved with gardening in containers is watering. Container gardens make it possible for people who can no longer do a lot of bending or heavy digging—but can still wield a hose or a watering can—to continue to experience the joys of gardening. In addition, children or new gardeners can learn some of the basics of gardening by maintaining a container garden.

Creating container gardens with style calls for an understanding of how containers work in the landscape and a careful evaluation of the proposed site. Then the right containers must be selected and matched with suitable plants. Containers come in an endless variety of shapes, sizes, and materials. While not all plants can be grown in containers, many are good candidates. This book includes special chapters on the best container plants from the major plant groups: annuals, perennials, bulbs, vegetables, herbs, roses, shrubs, trees, and tropicals.

Arranging plants effectively in containers requires a knowledge of growth requirements and complementary forms, textures, and colors. A single plant or more than one of the same plant makes an impact, as will a more complex grouping of several different plants. Whether you create a parterre herb garden, a colorful window box display, a foliage composition, or a single dramatic focal point, you will soon develop an eye for what you like and what works in your garden.

To be successful with container gardening, you must use quality potting soil and match the right potting mix with the right plant and pot. Once you learn to recognize key ingredients on quality soil mix labels, you will take a lot of the guesswork out of container gardening. You can also learn how to mix your own soil; a potting soil recipe is included for you to follow (see page 50).

Selecting healthy transplants and planting them properly is easy if you know a few tricks to planting in containers, such as ensuring that the drainage hole is not blocked and that the container is not too full of soil. While container gardens are faster and easier to establish than other kinds of gardens, they depend on you more than do plants in the ground for soil, fertilizer, and water. You can't forget about them, even for a short time, as you can plants in the ground, which draw moisture and nutrients from the soil.

You may be surprised at how many plants can be grown in containers—for flowers, foliage, fragrance, edible goodness, or all of these. As the following pages reveal, gardening in containers opens the door to new possibilities for creative expression.

Simple containers of flowers or herbs—such as these with sage and zinnias—create a miniature garden.

Containers in the Landscape

This well-placed container of begonias and lantana marks the corner of these brick steps.

The possibilities for containers in your garden are almost limitless. They can provide spots of color, serve as accents, or become the focal point for a particular area. Simply look around your landscape and let your imagination lead you to discovering locations that will benefit from decorative accents for containers. Then evaluate your chosen sites to determine how to best adapt your containers to these.

Determining the Functions of Containers

Like any other garden feature, containers must serve a purpose rather than just being haphazardly placed in the landscape. That reason may be decorative or functional, but it should be well thought out in order for the containers to look as if they belong. Containers work magic in the landscape. They can be delightfully ornamental, accenting other plants or features or drawing the eye to a focal point in the garden. They can be purely practical, creating space on a hard surface, such as a patio, for a productive herb or vegetable garden. Or they can be refreshingly seasonal, providing color throughout the year.

You will find many ways to use containers once you discover their beauty and function.

Colorful wax begonias in clay bowls provide the finishing touch in this courtyard, brightening the green plantings and placing emphasis on the arbor-covered center of the garden.

Add Color and Style

As is true when decorating the interior spaces of your home, you need to accessorize your outdoor locations to provide that final touch. Look around your landscape to assess areas where the brightening effect of potted flowers or the softening impact of foliage in a pot would make all the difference. A critical ingredient in choosing finishing touches is individual taste. If you have a favorite color or container, start with these elements and build your final design around them.

Magnets of color. One of the best uses of containers in the landscape is as colorful, visual pointers. They attract attention to entrances, to stopping places, and to other interesting spots on the property. Pots of color can help direct visitors to a door or down a hidden path that leads them to a delightful resting place.

Color attracts the eye, and the brighter the color, the more quickly the eye is drawn to it. A handsome container brimming with red foliage or flowers says, "Stop and look!" Bright yellow signals the need to slow down, perhaps for a step, a turn, or the end of a walk. Likewise, soft colors and combinations of green foliage convey a feeling of serenity. White, blue, silver, soft pink, and pastel yellow are quieter in a pot but will still draw attention to a particular point of interest.

Accents. In the world of design, accents bring out the beauty of an existing scene. Containers act as this design element as they combine their elegant form with the lush color in plants. The perfect touch of color provides an immediate impact, especially when the background is a monochromatic one, such as an all-evergreen planting, a wall, or a fence.

Paying special attention to texture, you can also use foliage compositions to wake up a setting; to temper the hardness of a step, a house corner, the edge of a wall, or a windowsill; or to soften flat paved areas. By mixing interesting colors and textures in a single pot, you create a minigarden that is an attraction in itself.

Containers, when placed in just the right spot, become furnishings that add balance, serve as a visual anchor in the landscape, and highlight noteworthy features.

Planted with geraniums and Swedish ivy, lush window boxes tucked onto ledges add bright colors and greenery to a vine-covered courtyard wall.

This cone-shaped boxwood with its underplanting of variegated ivy and dwarf boxwood serves as a miniature parterre garden accent at a home's entryway.

Containers in the Landscape

A chimney pot of cascading white petunias is the focal point of this patio. The planting of verbena at the foot ties the container to the surrounding landscape.

Focal points. Imagine seeing at the end of a lane an intriguing shape, a movement, or a brilliant flash of color, one that seems to beckon you. That is the goal of a focal point: to draw you into the heart of the garden or to some other special place at the end of your line of vision. There may be several locations in your landscape suitable for placement of a main feature. Look for horizontal lines that need breaking up and for places with an empty space.

A focal point may be part of a framed view through a window, a gate, a door, or an arbor. Because of their sculptural qualities, containers serve well as the center of attention. Once you have decided on a site, look around for appropriate containers for your plants. Some inspired choices are beautifully designed antique containers, pots, and artifacts. (If you are going to blow your budget, this may be the one place to do it.)

Fillers in borders. Containers make it easy to add plants to a flower border without disturbing the basic plantings. The colors and the textures of the border can be enhanced with the forms and the colors of the containers. To highlight an unusual plant, place it in a container rather than in the ground where it may be overshadowed by neighboring plants.

When planning a party or other special event, look to potted plants as part of the decoration. They can serve as fillers or be repotted with other plants. For instance, soft pastels and whites produce a romantic air for a wedding in the garden at night. Change the mood completely with sparkling hot colors for a child's birthday celebration. You can even install tropical plants into your existing garden for a summer luau.

These containers of black mondo and seasonal blooms add color, texture, and form to an existing bed.

Create Instant Gardens

Containers can create a garden—instantly—where one might not be possible otherwise. Wherever there are hard surfaces, or just hard soil, use containers to supply the friendly environment needed for plant roots to thrive.

Space savers. If space is at a premium in your vegetable garden, plants in pots can provide a solution. You will be surprised at how many salads you can get out of a barrel of lettuce. In the summer, the same pot can be used to grow a warm-weather crop, such as cherry tomatoes or purple basil. A container garden of tomatoes, peppers, herbs, or cut flowers that is located near the kitchen door makes snipping for a garnish or a bouquet a snap. Such a container garden can also be a fun summer project for children. You can easily grow beans in a container and train them on poles or arches. Children are amazed by these fast-growing vines and can occasionally be talked into having a healthful, freshly picked snack!

A pyramid of stacked terra-cotta pots creates a minigarden at the edge of a patio. (Left to right, bottom: leaf lettuce, sage, Red Russian kale, and rue; top: Leyland cypress, dusty miller, and mahonia)

Pots, especially large ones, define spaces in the landscape, outlining a seated area on a deck, a patio, or a sidewalk. Try using them to carve out a cozy spot in a wide open area, such as on a big deck or in an expansive lawn.

Portable gardens. One of the great advantages of growing plants in containers is that the pots do not have to stay in the same place all of the time. Feel free to move pots around to suit either fancy or function. Perhaps a container on a patio table is perfect for everyday but would be more safely situated elsewhere during a child's birthday party.

The portability of containers also allows you to relocate them to prime spots during the plant's peak periods of bloom. Other times, when the plants are more dormant, simply place the containers out of sight. Bring tender plants indoors if chilly weather threatens. Put large pots on dollies to roll them to new positions.

Portable containers are ideal for placing colorful annuals around a pool. (Left to right: geraniums, purslane, bougainvillea, zinnias, and blue daze)

Showcase Your Plants

Containers allow you to incorporate more plants or to add a strong accent into the design of a limited landscape. Use containers in tight places where it is not possible or practical to build a bed. Ordinary landscape plants, such as boxwood, often have more impact when set in containers because of the containers' architectural qualities. This is especially the case when you place good-sized nursery plants, such as those purchased in 5- to 15-gallon pots, in small gardens. For example, in a confined setting, one well-sited Little Gem magnolia in a handsome large container lends an air of permanence to almost any setting.

Maximum impact. Many gardeners love to collect interesting and unusual plants, which do not always have a lot in common visually. That is where containers help out, providing a unifying element of color and form that holds the grouping together. When creating a collection, group pots and give the grouping a space of its own. Using a French wire étagère or a baker's rack is an excellent and inexpensive way to display your favorite small plants.

In a small garden, containers give the impression of depth and greater mass, as do these two hibiscus trees flanking a doorway.

In the case of some plant groups, such as herbs, gardeners want at least one of each kind. Placing individual herbs in containers and displaying them as a collection eliminate the hodgepodge effect.

Expanded plant range. With container gardening, border and bed designs may incorporate plants that would not ordinarily be practical. Set out citrus, hibiscus, and other tropicals trained into the shape of a small tree right in the middle of daylilies and daffodils for a summer-only treat. Or grow rot-prone lavender in a fast-draining clay pot that re-creates the conditions of its native Mediterranean region. By putting pots to work, you will have a greater range of plant and design choices. With some plants, the containers may be sunk so that the rims are nearly level with the surrounding grade and mulch, and the need for water is reduced. The plants will look like a permanent installation, yet you will be able to move the pots out of the garden and into a greenhouse or inside your home for the winter.

Screens and sculpture. Several containers in a row create a miniscreen wherever you need one. Evergreens, such as ligustrum and camellia, are ideal for screens. Or use one or more containers with trellises in them to grow espaliered plants, such as sasanqua camellia or the fast-growing English ivy. Add annual vines for extra interest and color during the summer.

Containers themselves can be statuesque, especially large or unique ones. Highly decorative antique containers and interesting shaped pots attract attention in the same way that a sculpture does. Use them as focal points in beds, in an herb garden, on a terrace, or anywhere you want an architectural accent.

Certain containers lend themselves to atypical uses. For example, grow clinging plants on shapely containers to create a leafy sculpture. Or set a pot on its side in a flowerbed and place adjacent plants so that they appear to be spilling out of it. You can even convert a container into a fountain or a water garden. Or set a container upside down as a base for another container or as a pedestal for an ornament, such as a gazing ball or a sundial.

Finding Locations for Containers

The joy of gardening in containers comes in part from matching the right plants and containers to the right sites. Look around the outside of your house for spots where containers will add a graceful or whimsical touch or where you want to have plants but gardening directly in the ground is not possible. The obvious places to start are with the architectural extensions of your home; then move out from there to areas in your landscape that need colorful or dramatic accents.

This statuesque clay pot becomes a fountain with the addition of a recirculating pump; set in a water garden, its rich earth tones and comely lines serve to accent the entire planting.

The addition of a large pot of pink impatiens is all that is needed to break the horizontal lines on this deck. The repetition of flowers used elsewhere in the garden ties this design together.

Enhance Your Home's Exterior

In determining placement of containers, start with the more obvious architectural elements of your home, such as the walkways and steps, entryways, decks or patios, and porches. Many homes also have the perfect windowsill or balcony for a window box or other container. Dress up these locations instantaneously with the judicious choice of containers and plants.

Walkways and steps. Along walkways and on steps, container gardens not only are pretty but also can help maintain safety. Place containers to mark a change in grade or a step up or down. (When setting containers on succeeding steps, be sure to place the tallest plants on the topmost step.) Use containers to signal sudden drop-offs or as a sort of wall along the edge of an elevated terrace where

A variety of containers filled with (left to right) verbena, dianthus, alyssum, and petunias directs visitors down the steps to a seating area.

Containers around an entry create an inviting approach to the door. This group, which features a Little Gem magnolia, caladiums, and white impatiens, accents the dove gray coloring of the house.

there is not enough height to merit a railing. Fill oversize pots with small trees or tree-form shrubs to create a canopy and underplant with a colorful carpet of flowers.

Entryways. At an entryway, a well-placed container accentuates the best features of the doorway. Echo the color of the door with plants. Look at the entryway from afar to ensure that the placement you are considering works well with the entire landscape. The container and its plants should reflect or contrast with the colors in the plantings and with any hard surfaces. Carefully select a container or a plant stand to complement decorative architectural features of the entry. In areas where the containers must be low (in front of windows, for example), use plants that grow outward and develop a rounded shape.

To accentuate the entry at night, consider uplighting a carefully placed potted tree or shrub. If a prominent tree or shrub is planted on one side of the entry, a large-container planting set closer to the door provides balance. This will also help lead the eye to the entryway.

Porches and decks. Plants in containers on a porch or a deck help link the structure to the landscape. Pinpoint the places where container plantings can soften hard edges and angles. Then consider the background for the container garden. Depending on the approach to the porch or the deck, the background may be architectural or natural. Most decks that are approached from inside the house will have a view of a textured green background. In the case of a porch that is usually viewed from the street or from a parking area, the color and the texture of the house's exterior dominate. Therefore, choose containers and plants that stand out from these backgrounds.

With its sense of enclosure, a porch is a traditional home for pots and hanging baskets of ferns, which add vertical interest and color, softening the hard edges of the area.

Windowsills and window boxes. Window boxes add charm to almost every windowsill. They may be anything from homemade wooden boxes to steel hayracks lined with coco fiber liners. Window boxes are particularly visible, so it's important that you keep them well groomed. If you have a dark-colored house, plant flowers that contrast sharply with it. Variegated or gray foliage also stands out. On the other hand, if you have a light-colored house, use plants with dark foliage or deep- or hot-colored flowers to make the window boxes show up better. In very sunny locations, light-colored flowers create an uncomfortable glare.

Impatiens do well in window boxes that are shaded during the afternoon. Their red color accents the cool colors of the house.

Wherever the plants are placed, be sure that you can get water to them. Elevated plants dry out faster because of increased air circulation and restricted root space.

Balconies and rooftops. On balconies, use plantings that extend through the railing. Place containers so that when you are on the balcony, you have a feeling of privacy but are also able to enjoy the view. A screen of shrubs or vines wrapped through the railing may be what is needed.

Potted trees give some protection from the sun. Choose trees, such as crepe myrtle, that have broad, spreading canopies. Trees with dense foliage provide more shade. One good choice is citrus trees, which also have fragrant flowers that are particularly pleasant in warmer areas. Maple trees, which can be grown where citrus trees cannot, cast an excellent shade and have brilliantly colored foliage in the fall. Do not place a container where a child could climb up on it and fall over the rail.

Tropical vines, flowing plants that fill gaps in railings, and small trees are all excellent choices for an intimate balcony.

In a courtyard garden, groupings of pots can highlight a feature against a wall, such as this fountain, and give the setting a feeling of depth. Here, espaliered ivy breaks the monotony of the wall.

Accenting Your Landscape

Because containers are so versatile and portable, you'll not want to overlook other locations in your landscape or garden that need an accent. Pay particular attention to those areas that allow you to garden in an otherwise unsuitable site. The simple fact is that you can use containers almost anywhere to provide you with year-round gardens.

In front of walls. When a privacy wall or the side of a house looks blank and one-dimensional, break the expanse with container plantings of small trees, sprawling shrubs, or climbing vines. Ornate pots are even more elegant when sited against a plain surface, such as a stucco wall. Brick walls, though generally of one color, have a texture. Simple pots usually look best in front of such walls.

Concrete is also a good choice for use against brick because light plays well on details of concrete pots, casting interesting shadows. Also, concrete containers pick up the light color of the mortar while at the same time contrast with the overall color of the brick.

Use containers to highlight a feature of a wall, such as a fountain, a plaque, or a portal. Groupings of pots create dimension in front of a wall. Try combining many plants to create a miniature garden.

Potted topiary junipers accent a tiered fountain against a brick wall, creating a simple but elegant look.

Patios and pool areas. Such outdoor entertaining areas are extensions of living space. The flooring of patios and pools, however, can seem an unending flat landscape. Attractively planted containers define the boundaries and visually connect these spaces to the surrounding garden and the house.

Drought-tolerant wax begonias and ornamental grasses do well in shallow, bowl-shaped pots.

Courtyards. Rarely do courtyards contain lines from walls and hedges that make clean backdrops for colorful plantings in containers. The same design considerations used in open spaces apply to courtyards. Look for focal points and ways to soften corners. Select plants that are in scale and provide balance. Because of the shadows cast by walls and hedges, some areas of courtyards can be dark. Brighten up such a space with liberal use of light colors—plants that flower or have white, silver-gray, or lime green variegated foliage are good choices. Impatiens, caladium, and variegated ivy all do well in containers and bring patches of white into the garden. The containers themselves, if light-colored, also make the courtyard appear brighter.

Courtyards often have a warm microclimate, one that permits you to grow some tender, fragrant plants, such as gardenia or jasmine. Scented plants have more impact in these enclosed areas. Even one small plant such as a gardenia perfumes the entire courtyard.

Select white or light-colored flowers, such as impatiens and petunias, and variegated foliage to brighten a courtyard garden.

Arbors. Dress up an arbor with plain posts, using containers filled with billowing plants and set at the base of each post. For variety, choose plants of a different texture than those growing on the arbor. Use containers to limit the reach of vigorous vines growing on an arbor. Contain a vine such as wisteria in a large pot, which will help constrict its roots.

A pair of containers filled with dwarf hibiscus and asparagus ferns softens this arbor's columns.

Gazebos. Hanging baskets of ferns or trailing flowers in containers are excellent additions to a gazebo. If hanging baskets are likely to block a pretty view, mount L-shaped hangers on the posts of the gazebo and hang baskets from them. The baskets frame the view from both within and without. Railing hangers allow containers to act as a sort of bunting for the gazebo. Plan your container gardening accordingly. Think ahead to times when you will entertain in the gazebo. For an Independence Day party, plant a pot of scarlet salvia, silvery dusty miller, and blue and white petunias to create a patriotic mood. Another good place to feature containers around a gazebo is at the entrance. Floor space in a gazebo is usually at a premium, limiting the number of containers that you can use. Large plantings at the entrance balance the void of flora inside.

Utility areas. Every part of the garden offers an opportunity for exercising creativity. Work-related utility areas are especially good places for experimenting with plant combinations and design ideas because these spots are less visible. Are there some favorite flowers that

To match the style of this romantic Victorian gazebo, choose full, ornate plantings, such as these ferns that flow out of detailed stone urns.

When paired with a rustic olive jar, old-fashioned hollyhocks make a weathered shed an inviting part of the garden.

you want to return every year from seed? Sow them in a pot around the garden shed. Do you have a striking container that is chipped or otherwise unsuitable for holding plants? Display it as a piece of sculpture. One of the delights of a garden is unexpected pretty pictures in the landscape.

Evaluating the Site

You need to consider the horticultural needs of container plants as well as the specific requirements of their locations. In addition to design considerations, a site must work from a practical standpoint; therefore, it is important to understand the physical conditions of the area you have selected. Once you have evaluated the site, you have the information necessary to choose containers and plants that are most suitable for it.

The shade cast by a large backyard tree makes this a perfect spot for containers of shade-loving caladium and bromeliads.

A small window box of ivy, Johnny-jump-ups, ornamental kale, primrose, and ornamental grass is more easily maintained in the spring than in the summer when the weather is often hot and dry.

Understand the Physical Needs

Always remember that containers are artificial environments and that the plants in them are subject to more stress than are plants growing in the ground. Temperature extremes are more likely to cause damage, because the soil mass is relatively small and exposed. Soil in a pot naturally dries out more quickly than soil in the ground and winds—even gentle ones—cause drying not only through the foliage but through the surface of porous pots, such as those made of clay. The sun heats both the containers and the hard surfaces around them, literally cooking sensitive plants. (Turn to the section beginning on page 59 to help you select container plants that are suited to specific environments.)

These environmental conditions of wind, sun, and tempera ture, plus such factors as humidity and exposure to water, produce a multitude of small microclimates, which create quite different growing conditions even in a small area. For example, an exposed patio supports only those plants capable of withstanding intense heat, extreme cold, and drying winds. A sheltered corner with a southeastern exposure is often the ideal location for tender plants. You can expect very shady, low places to have a moist, cool microclimate.

A grouping of containers has its own microclimate and can protect other plants from sun or drying wind. Make a microclimate right on top of the soil surface with mulch. Spanish moss, soil conditioner, shredded pine, cypress bark, or small pinecones all make attractive mulches that conserve soil moisture.

When choosing locations for your containers, consider that the plants will need to be watered almost daily in the summer. Put a window box where you can easily reach it. The site must be accessible to watering, whether you use a hose, a sprinkler, or a watering can.

Also, think about your gardening habits. When just one container is filled with plants, carrying a watering can to the container is not difficult. However, with an extensive container garden, watering becomes a time-consuming, tedious burden. (See pages 53 and 54 for suggestions on how to keep the soil mix in your containers moist longer.)

Place your containers within a hose's reach of a spigot. It will make watering a much more pleasant task.

Choose the Correct Shape, Size, and Number of Containers

The surrounding elements in a setting help you decide the shape, the size, and the number of containers that will look best. By either contrasting or imitating existing garden characteristics, the containers become a supporting element of the garden design. If the nearby shapes are vertical (for example, existing plants, benches, or fences), select a rounded container for contrast. Should fine textures and softness predominate, strike a bold note by using a container that is square or triangular or that has a glazed surface. Sometimes, imitation helps to accent a particular feature of the landscape. For instance, a rounded pot reflects the shape of a prized old boxwood that is in view elsewhere. In general, select the largest container possible for ease of care. But keep the overall scene in mind: A small pot

An urn filled with pansies and sweet alyssum creates vertical interest atop a column covered with a potato vine.

Set containers along a walkway in a place where they allow plenty of clearance for walking.

is lost when surrounded by a massive planting, a big house, or any considerable structure. And a huge pot looks completely out of place if the planting in which it is placed is not substantial enough to balance it.

When placing containers, leave enough room around them to walk by comfortably. Otherwise, foliage and flowers can stain your clothing, or the plants may be damaged. Consider the eventual spread of the plants, too. Do not allow the containerized plants to spread more than 3 to 4 inches into a path. Plants with foliage that emits a fragrance when slightly crushed or touched (such as rosemary or pineapple sage) are exempt from this rule since brushing against the leaves has a pleasing result. Little-used walkways should be at least 18 inches wide. Frequently used walkways should be kept clear enough for two people to walk abreast, about 4 feet wide. In narrow areas, choose upright containers rather than broad, bowl-shaped ones to help ensure clear and safe passage.

By looking at the shape of the site, you can quickly conclude how many containers are needed. To fill a corner (a triangular shape), one large pot or three small to medium-sized pots will generally be sufficient. For a large corner, add more pots.

When grouped together, three small upright containers create a miniature flowerbed of New Guinea hybrid impatiens in a tight space.

Always use an odd number of containers; otherwise, the eye will focus on the most central space between the containers.

Of paramount importance are balance and scale. For balance, set out two containers or two sets of containers when flanking a space, such as a walkway, a bench, or an entry. In addition, balance a design with containers by choosing pots of the proper scale, even if you use an unequal number of pots on each side. Asymmetrical balance is achieved by equal mass not by an equal number of pots. For example, place one large pot, perhaps with a tall plant, on one side and a group of three pots with lower plantings on the other side.

Read further for suggestions on selecting the appropriate containers for your specific needs.

Groups of two or two sets of containers make a balanced composition when flanking a wall or an entry.

Choosing the Right Container

Terra-cotta pots are a favorite with gardeners and come in all shapes and sizes.

When deciding on a particular container, think about its size, shape, and function and how well it reflects your personal style.

With so many charming pots in garden shops, it is tempting to buy the first one you like. However, charm is only one reason to buy a pot. When selecting a container, think first about function and form. The container should be the right size and shape for the plant and the site; it must also drain well. And it will last longer if it is made of weatherproof materials. In many instances, weight and portability are important. After considering these criteria, look at the variety of forms available and decide which best complements your home and garden style.

Function Before Beauty

You create a small habitat for a plant when you put it in a pot. Once you choose a particular site for the pot, you give the plant its own microclimate. For the plant to function well in this setting, the pot must meet certain requirements. Before you purchase a pot, you should know what to look for in a container.

Size and Shape

A lot of failures arise from trying to grow a plant in a pot of the wrong size. If the container is too small, the plant may topple over, become root bound, dry out too quickly, or languish and not bloom or develop properly. By contrast, if the pot is too large, the soil holds water too long, and the plant's roots will rot. The permanent container should be approximately 5 inches wider in diameter than the root ball (or the nursery pot).

Shape is also important. The basic classic clay pot, which includes the shape of urns and strawberry jars, is ideal for most plants. It allows room for roots to grow deep and exposes less soil to the air, thus limiting dehydration. Dishes, window boxes, and hanging baskets are fine for growing shallow-rooted plants in the spring or in the fall, when the sunlight is less intense and not as much watering is required. These shallow containers also work well in the shade or with drought-tolerant species, such as cacti and succulents. If you use a shallow container in full sunlight in the summer, select the widest one possible without it looking oversize; be prepared to water often.

Drainage and Moisture Retention

All containers need drainage holes, or the plants in the pots will rot and die. If you convert an unusual object, such as a wheelbarrow, a wooden box, or a watering can into a plant container, put several small holes or one large hole in the bottom of it. From time to time, make sure water is draining properly. While the pot must have proper drainage, it should also not dry out too quickly. Containers made of porous materials, such as clay or concrete, absorb some water and may dry out slightly faster than plastic or metal containers.

Hardy ice plant, sedum, and hen-and-chicks thrive in full sunlight; their upright but mounding forms accent the urn's curving lines.

A chimney flue serves as a receptacle for a basket of lantana. Be sure any such containers fashioned from unusual objects allow for good drainage.

25

Inexpensive clay pots are prone to chipping and cracking when the moisture in the clay freezes and thaws in the winter. Pots of better quality will last longer.

Weather Tolerance

In the winter, when water in a pot freezes and thaws continuously, the pot may chip and crack. Clay, concrete, and foam pots are particularly prone to do this. The better the quality of the pot, the longer the pot endures outdoors. Clay or concrete pots last longer if they sit on feet; this promotes drainage and keeps the pots from standing in water. Some gardeners use prized clay or concrete pots as cachepots and bring the pots indoors in the winter to avoid damage. (See page 57 for details.) If you garden in a cold climate and do not want to take any chances, select a pot made of materials that do not freeze, such as metal, plastic, stone, or wood. Some grades of terra-cotta are more tolerant of freezing temperatures than others, but it is almost impossible to distinguish them in a store, as they are rarely guaranteed. Mexican pottery is usually the least resistant to cold.

Weight and Portability

It is surprising how heavy a container filled with plants and soil mix can be, especially after a watering. An already heavy container made of clay, concrete, lead, or stone increases the overall weight of the planting. Some containers, such as window boxes and hanging baskets, must be lightweight so that they can be easily suspended and supported. In some cases, you may prefer a lighter container. You can lift it easily and move it indoors for the winter if it contains a plant

A moss-lined wire basket does not add much weight to this planting of petunias, geraniums, and sweet alyssum. It is perfect for use as a standing container or for suspending overhead.

such as a tropical palm. Conversely, some pots made from foam or plastic are too lightweight for large plants, such as trees and shrubs. Adding a layer of gravel to the bottom of a container anchors it and keeps the plant from toppling in the wind.

One of the best ways to make a container more portable is to set it on casters. This enables you to move the plant around easily and to take advantage of changing seasons and light patterns. For example, you might want to move some containers to catch the morning sunlight (an eastern exposure) so that plants do not blister in the western afternoon sun. In the winter, you may wish to move some plants to a sheltered area behind a south-facing wall or next to the house where they do not receive the full force of northern winds. If casters are too expensive for a large collection, you can always use a small hand truck to help you move plants indoors for the winter.

Suitable Materials

Containers come in a wide variety of materials, each with advantages and disadvantages. Knowing these in advance will help you make good selections.

Clay. The traditional favorite, clay offers a classic look that works in formal or informal gardens. Its rich, earthy color adds warmth to any planting. A collection of clay pots can tie a disparate group of plants together. Clay also breathes, which means plants in clay containers are less likely to suffer from overwatering—a plus when wintering prize plants indoors.

Clay has only two drawbacks. Because clay is porous, the potting mix in a container made of this material dries out more quickly in full sunlight in the summer; this can be a problem if the pot is so small that the soil dries out in an afternoon. And inexpensive clay pots are prone to chipping in the winter in areas where temperatures drop below freezing. Still, many gardeners feel the pluses of clay outweigh the minuses. You can coat the inside of the clay pot with a water sealant or a rubber compound, or just slip in a plastic liner to reduce moisture loss through the sides (take care not to block drainage holes).

Brimming with petunias, Johnny-jump-ups, and lavender, this traditional clay pot has taken on an attractive mossy patina with age, lending an established look to the garden.

Choosing the Right Container

Good plastic pots are tough, tolerate freezing and thawing, and retain moisture well. Many gardeners prefer them for plants grown in full sunlight, such as these rosemary plants.

White Madagascar periwinkle looks cool and refreshing in contrast to a concrete planter.

Plastic. Economical, durable, and lightweight, plastic is among the most practical of all container materials. It does not absorb moisture, which is an advantage in the summer. Because it is lightweight, plastic is often the material of choice for containers for large shrubs and trees. (Add gravel to the bottom of plastic pots to counterbalance the weight of the top growth of shrubs and trees.) Gardeners who once eschewed plastic for aesthetic reasons have found that many of today's plastic pots are such good imitations of clay and stone that it is hard to tell the difference. Quality plastic is durable and tolerant of freezing; however, cheap plastic becomes brittle after a few years.

Concrete. Stonelike concrete has an elegant presence in the garden and is at home in formal settings. It typically comes in gray or white, but it can also be found in colors that make it resemble old copper or lead. Concrete is relatively porous and absorbs water, which may cause potting mix to dry out more quickly. Cheaper grades are subject to cracking and freeze damage in colder areas. Like clay, concrete can acquire a handsome aged appearance.

Foam. Lightweight and inexpensive, foam containers have won a lot of converts. Made of synthetic materials, these containers are poured, molded, and tinted to look like clay or concrete, but they are more portable and do not freeze. Quality, however, is important; cheaper pots are prone to chipping and flaking.

Wood. Wooden containers range from old-fashioned half-barrels to elegant English-style planter boxes. They can be expensive or inexpensive, depending on the type of wood used, the design, and the construction. Planters made of thick wood insulate plant roots well. Choose a naturally rot-resistant wood, such as cedar or cypress, or one treated with a nontoxic preservative (especially if you are growing edibles, such as vegetables or herbs). Screws and other metal appendages should be rustproof.

Metal. Metal containers—such as those made of iron, lead, or steel—are generally heavy, durable, and nonporous. Aluminum containers are an exception in that they are lightweight. Once the preferred material for decorative urns and planters, metal has been replaced by less expensive materials. It is still used as a supporting framework for lined metal window boxes, hanging baskets, topiary forms, and trellises. Because they blend well with historic houses and antiques, metal containers are good for cottage, English, or period gardens. Metal is cold in the winter and hot in the summer and is subject to corrosion and rust if not given a protective coating. Plants in metal containers will bake if placed in full summer sunlight.

Weatherproof wood is a good material to use in the construction of custom containers, such as this planter that features gerbera daisies, kalanchoe, ivy, and other plants.

This grouping of pots and a large shallow dish holds a mix of paperwhites, ornamental kale, pansies, and trailing ivy.

Variety of Forms

Let your individual style come into play in your choice of pots. Like interior furnishings, containers are available in a wide variety of forms to suit an assortment of personal tastes. Some containers are identified by particular eras or schools of design. Urns often have a distinct Greek or French flair. Highly ornate pots may reflect the Victorian era. Clay pots are classics for the cottage garden style. Clean lines and asymmetrical shapes suggest contemporary or perhaps Japanese styling. The most critical ingredients in choosing containers are the style of your home and individual taste, as decorative touches are facets of a gardener's personality.

Plant a miniature herb garden in a strawberry jar, which is as sculptural as it is functional.

Pick a Classic

The pot has been a garden fixture for centuries. It is excellent for growing a specimen plant or for arranging several plants in a colorful composition. Always tapered or box shaped, the classic pot meets the requirements of a variety of plant types. It adds height to any planting and coordinates with many different garden styles. A large pot can function as a small raised bed, lifting plants up to better display their blooms or to provide easier access. A pot can be plain and simple, or it can be fluted, rimmed, or molded in many decorative ways. It can be used singly, in groups, in lines, as an accent, or as a focal point.

Dishes Create Horizontal Lines

Stable, shallow dishes are short bowls that add a restful element to the garden. They are especially attractive when located in an area where their circular forms can be viewed from above or when different sizes are grouped together. Dishes provide a lot of surface area for mixed plantings. Use them to feature low-mounding plants and trailers and for shallow-rooted and drought-tolerant plants, such as succulents and cacti.

Jars Draw the Eye Upward

Jars—standard, olive, wine, and strawberry—add vertical interest and graceful form to a garden, making lovely accents. Some jars are more ornamental than functional because they have little surface area at the top for plants; use these as sculpture. Strawberry jars, however, have a series of pockets for planting, which allows you to build a tower of plants. The larger the jar, the more effective it is as a planter. Plant annuals, herbs, and succulents—as well as strawberries—in jars and water carefully, ensuring that the moisture filters down through all of the soil.

Urns Impart Old-world Charm

An urn resembles a pot on a pedestal. It calls attention in the garden, much as a vase of flowers does indoors. Urns have a classic, formal look and are frequently used in pairs as accents near entryways or on a column as the focal point at the center of a planting. They are

In an urn, use plants that reach upward and outward to complement the formal lines of a pot on a pedestal. Here, a billowing geranium, clothed in fancy foliage, marries well with a classical urn.

highly decorative and lend themselves both to fanciful mixtures of flowers and trailing plants and to simple plantings, such as a stylized ivy topiary, a bountiful scented geranium, or a frothy fern. Urns can be deep or shallow, and their depth affects the kind of plants you put in them; shallow ones have so little room for soil that you are limited to shallow-rooted, drought-tolerant plants, such as hen-and-chicks. Place urns in areas where they cannot be toppled. If placed atop a column, be sure the column is wide enough to support the urn.

Planter Boxes Solve Problems

Planter boxes are low, stable features that are used—among other ways—as accents, for spots of color in narrow horizontal spaces, and as low walls that define limits. They can be purchased, converted from old treasures, or custom-made to fit your needs. Large planter boxes function as a small raised bed and are especially well suited for apartments and rooftop gardens. You can grow a number of plants at once in planter boxes and spend less time on care and maintenance than you would if the plants were being grown in individual containers. Small planter boxes are versatile features, easily moved to take advantage of sunlight or shade. By using a liner inside a planter box, you can easily swap out plantings to change the display with the seasons. Always be sure there is plenty of room for clearance around any planters placed on the floor. Those that are set on deck or porch railings or on windowsills must be well supported.

Hanging Baskets Add Height

Classic summertime features, hanging baskets add height to a garden, sometimes appearing to float in the air. They bring flowers, ferns, and foliage plants to porches, gazebos, swings, and arbors. When planted with red salvia, petunias, or lantana, hanging baskets entice butterflies or hummingbirds up to the house or within sight of a window. (Even red flowers without nectar, such as geraniums and impatiens, attract hummingbirds to a nearby feeder.)

Some baskets, such as those made of wire or wooden slats, can be planted on the bottom and the sides, creating a lush tropical look. They must, however, be lined with sheet moss or coco fiber to contain the potting mix. Closed baskets are simpler to work with and have a saucer to catch water. This reservoir of water is an important feature because hanging baskets are shallow and the soil in them is prone to dehydration in the summer. Hang them in partial shade or

The fresh crispness of pink-and-white Madagascar periwinkle contrasts nicely with the natural handcrafted look of this planter box.

A moss basket filled with double impatiens, asparagus fern, and trailing ivy flourishes in the partial shade of a cedar arbor.

shield them from the afternoon sun. Remember that when hanging baskets are wet, they take on additional weight. When you mount a basket, take steps to securely fasten it overhead.

Wall-Mounted Planters Offer Welcome

Wall-mounted planters make charming accents for walls and allow you to maximize space in a small area, such as a balcony, a courtyard, or a narrow passageway. As a sign of welcome, mount a wall planter on the outside wall of a house near an entryway or on a fence, a door, or a post. Growing conditions are similar to those in hanging baskets. However, walls radiate heat, which extends the growing season. Like other small containers, wall planters require frequent watering. They are ideally suited for flowering bed plants, bulbs, ferns, and trailers, such as ivy. When plants are watered, the planter will be heavier, so be sure to attach the planter to the wall securely; take special pains with planters mounted on doors.

The cyclamen and pansies peeking from this wall-mounted planter— which is made of concrete with a faux lead finish—break up an otherwise dark surface and invite visitors into the garden.

A metal hayrack, here filled with petunias, mealy-cup sage, and a geranium, is an instant window box.

Window Boxes and Hayracks: Instant Charm

Window boxes and hayracks are horizontal planters that add color, texture, and seasonal interest to a residence. They can be used as a formal design feature or just for fun to improve the view from inside the house. Window boxes and hayracks are also useful for maximizing space or for creating miniature gardens for persons unable to go outside. Like wire baskets, hayracks need to be lined with sheet moss or coco fiber, which holds the potting soil. Also, be sure to use brackets or spacers to hang hayracks far enough away from the house so that the wet soil does not do damage. If the metal of the hayrack is not already coated to prevent rust, spray it with sealant.

Like other containers that are suspended, window boxes and hayracks have the potential to come loose and fall. Make sure they rest on a windowsill or are affixed to the house in a safe and permanent fashion. Check them regularly whenever you water, change plantings, or add new soil.

Converted Treasures Bring a Personal Touch

Use objects not originally intended to hold plants to add personality to the garden. Such treasures include wooden shoeshine boxes, aluminum coal scuttles, old iron fireplace grills, wooden or metal wagons, fertilizer spreaders, chimney pots, washtubs, watering cans, iron kettles, and old tree stumps, to name a few. Porosity and insulation values of these converted containers vary. However, all plant holders must have drainage holes, be big enough to contain the plants you want to put in them, and be durable enough to last at least as long as the plants chosen to grow there.

Converted treasures, such as this antique wagon, add a touch of whimsy to the garden. Use them as actual containers or as decorative cachepots for a collection of plants in containers, as was done with these potted mums.

Filled with lobelia, dusty miller, and geraniums, these window boxes rest securely on a windowsill.

Creating Containers with Style

These shade-loving ferns, caladium, impatiens, and variegated ivy combine for a smashing container garden that makes the best use of color, form, and texture.

Containers offer an easy way to add year-round color to your landscape as you can always have them filled with plants in bloom.

After you choose your containers and decide where to put them, you'll need to select the appropriate plants. Determine if the garden is to be temporary or permanent and also whether the plants to be featured give their best show in the sunlight or the shade. To help present plants and containers to their best advantage, utilize the basic design elements of balance, color, and repetition. Finally, plan ahead for containers whose displays change with each season.

Selecting Suitable Plants

Before you actually purchase plants, assess your gardening habits. One of the more important considerations is the amount of maintenance a plant requires. For example, evergreens—such as boxwood, yaupon holly, and juniper—are classic low-maintenance container plants. And, generally, containers in the shade need less watering; therefore, plants that thrive in less light are usually lower maintenance. By contrast, annual bedding plants provide lots of color but require daily watering in the summer and changing out with each season. As a rule, tender tropicals, roses, and vegetables also must have more attention.

Another decision to make at the outset is whether your container is to house a temporary or permanent planting. Annuals, biennials, and some perennials are short-term seasonal plantings that add variety to the garden, as are vegetables, herbs, tender bulbs, and tropicals. By contrast, ornamental grasses, vines, ferns, hosta, roses, trees, and shrubs are enduring features in the garden. Some permanent plants are deciduous and put on a seasonal foliage, flower, or berry show. Others are evergreen; these plants provide background and structure that do not change. Try anchoring your planting with one lasting feature—perhaps a foliage plant, shrub, or tree to give continuity to a seasonal display of annuals.

Evergreen plantings, such as this miniature parterre featuring a tree-form variegated English holly, do not have to be changed out every season. In the underplanting of this garden, variegated edging boxwood accents each corner, boxleaf euonymus links the corners, and pinks add seasonal color.

A long lasting perennial, such as pampas grass, works as a permanent feature in a container surrounded by colorful, seasonal annuals, such as petunias.

35

Drought-tolerant marigolds thrive in a strawberry jar, adding a spot of color to a kitchen garden in full sunlight.

Impatiens in containers prefer some shade in the summer, where they can be shielded from the wilting effects of the afternoon sunlight.

The chapters beginning on page 59 contain information on plants well suited to containers. Refer to the plant group charts for those plants that offer the most color, foliage, fruit, or fragrance. Make a list of possible choices and then see which ones best fit the site and the containers.

Container Plants for Sunlight or Shade

Look at the location you have chosen and narrow your selection of plants to those that would do well in the light conditions of the site. Here are some general guidelines to help you choose your plants.

Sunlight. Select tough plants for a sunny site. Look at drought-tolerant annuals such as geraniums and marigolds; perennials such as fountain grass and sedum; trees such as holly; succulents that include yucca; and all types of cacti. Almost all herbs, vegetables, and roses need full sunlight, but they need moisture as well.

Combinations for sunny sites. To take the edge off the heat, try an ornamental grass in cool colors, such as the silvery Miscanthus; Homestead Purple verbena; purple or lavender petunias; and variegated vinca. For a brighter look, plant a yellow-and-purple combo—yellow daylily and mealy-cup sage or yellow lantana with purple petunias.

Shade. For a shady or partially shady site, choose plants that maintain good form and color in the shade. Consider annuals such as impatiens and coleus; perennials such as ferns and hosta; mint, parsley, and other herbs; leafy vegetables such as lettuce and spinach; bulbs such as caladium; English ivy, vinca, and other adaptable plants; and shade-tolerant shrubs and trees such as andromeda, leucothoe, magnolia, Japanese maple, and wax myrtle.

Once you have a handle on what grows well in shade, try your hand at creating interesting combinations of colors and textures.

Combinations for shady sites. A white-and-green combination of variegated ivy, white caladium, white impatiens, and maidenhair fern creates a sophisticated effect. Add pink caladium, impatiens, or wax begonias for impact. For more color, try a yellow-and-purple mix of chartreuse hosta, chartreuse coleus, purple or lavender impatiens, and sword fern (a tropical plant treated as an annual).

Cool-Weather or Warm-Weather Plants

It is important to learn in which seasons certain plants thrive, produce, or put on their showiest displays. The charts for each plant group indicate which plants are cool-weather plants and which are warm-weather plants. While permanent plants, such as shrubs and trees, are not classified this way, their showiest seasons are specified. Take advantage of the cool seasons of spring and fall to grow annual herbs or bedding plants, vegetables, or biennials in containers. In the spring or the fall, grow such cool-weather annuals as dianthus, Johnny-jump-ups, nasturtiums, ornamental cabbage and kale, pansies, and snapdragons. Or plant a cool-weather herb-and-salad garden of cilantro, dill, lettuce, parsley, radishes, and spinach.

In the summer, showcase heat-tolerant annuals, such as basil, marigold, peppers, tomatoes, verbena, and zinnia. Also good for warm-weather containers are permanent plantings of tender tropicals, succulents, and Mediterranean herbs, such as rosemary and sage. In the winter, you'll need cold-hardy evergreen herbs, perennials, trees, and shrubs. Try a planting of an herb, such as thyme, or a perennial, such as Lenten rose. Leyland cypress and camellias also do well in cold weather.

An underplanting of evergreen ivy and cool-weather annuals, such as lettuce and pansies, provides a finishing touch to this tree-form camellia.

Understanding Basic Design Elements

Understanding a few basic design considerations, such as balance, color, and repetition, helps you create plantings in containers that are not only attractive but also work well in the landscape.

Balance

Objects in a composition look more pleasing if they are visually balanced. Thus, in container gardening the container and its plant or plants should

A large terra-cotta planter is balanced with a mound of impatiens and plectranthus, a trailing Blackie sweet potato vine, and airy blades of lemon grass.

This perfectly balanced composition is achieved by repeating the combination of ferns and impatiens and the angular lines of the chimney pot form. The potted pink impatiens at the foot give a finished look.

not be too small for the site, or the planting will appear skimpy; nor should the planting overwhelm the space. Beware the spindly chimney pot planted with a too-tall tree or shrub; even if the pot is securely anchored, the planting will appear top-heavy. A vertical container of this type benefits from a cascading plant. With large broad pots or planters, the challenge is to keep the planting from appearing too low and too heavy. Improve a horizontal planter filled with spreading plants by adding taller accent plants.

When you place containers in the landscape, they should appear balanced with each other as well. If you flank a door with containers, set them as though you were balancing a scale. Place two of the same kind of plantings on each side for a formal symmetrical effect; or for an informal look, set several groups of pots (perhaps including a hanging basket) on one side to visually balance the weight of a large pot on the other.

Color

Colors can create optical illusions, alter the way you feel, and affect the apparent temperature in the garden landscape. Warm colors (red, orange, and yellow) create excitement and attract attention. They are energizing. Because they are bright, they catch the eye first, often pulling a scene or a vignette forward. This has the effect of making a large garden seem smaller and cozier and of making distant objects appear closer. Cool colors (purple, blue, and green) are restful and calming. They seem to recede, thus making a small space seem larger.

Color wheel. To use this color wheel, cut a small equilateral triangle of paper and position it on the wheel so that its points are on the three primary colors—red, yellow, and blue. As you rotate the triangle, the points show trios of complementary colors that work well together, making it easy for you to group flowers of corresponding colors. Choose a color scheme to your liking; then put together several different combinations of plants at the garden shop before making your purchase. For maximum impact in a small container, use shades of the same color family, such as blues, purples, and lavenders, instead of buying plants in a rainbow of colors.

Flowers and foliage should suit the color of the container and its background. Neutral backgrounds, including green leaves, a white fence, or bare wood, show off whites and all colors to equal advantage.

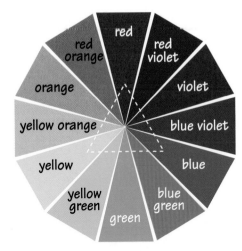

Color Wheel

The wheel is an artist's tool for previewing the impact of certain color combinations. It helps simplify color selection.

Planting a small container with flowers of a single bright color, such as the hot pink of this verbena, is a simple task that produces eye-catching results.

Using the same kind of flower in more than one color, such as with these pansies, is an easy way to combine plants in a small container for any season.

However, keep in mind that a red brick wall or a strong house paint color is difficult to match. Be wary of colors that are similar but do not quite harmonize. A red rose clashes against a red brick wall; a white or yellow flower is more pleasing.

Color strategies. If you find color confusing when planning a container garden, keep things simple. Below are a few strategies for working with color.

White. Elegant and fresh, white is a neutral that works with almost anything. It is the most visible color at night; if you like to enjoy your garden after hours, consider planting white flowers, such as petunias. White also works well in shade. White impatiens and variegated ivy, for example, will brighten any dark corner.

Soft versus strong colors. For a soft, pretty look, try a monochromatic scheme of one color family—bright yellow to pale yellow to creamy white; rich maroon to pale pink to white; or purple to lavender to white. For a bold accent, use red or bright pink, which will draw attention to a garden feature or attract hummingbirds or butterflies to your feeder. Add yellow to a container to wake up cool blue, purple, and green color schemes.

Related colors. Another easy way to blend colors is to use related colors—two, three, or four colors that are adjacent on the

MIX YOUR OWN PANSIES

Draw a dominant color from your house or garden and use it to put together a colorful container of three or more different types of pansies. Because pansies come in such a vast array of solid and contrasting blends, they are an ideal plant to mix and match. Here are a few suggested combinations to get you started, but don't hesitate to choose your own favorite pansy and build a color scheme around it.

Blue-Lavender Blend	Brick Red Blend	Warm Color Blend	Mauve-Rose Blend
Crystal Blend True Blue	Crystal Bowl Yellow	Crown Rose	Accord Rose with Blotch
Crystal Bowl Purple	Majestic Giants Red	Imperial Antique Shades	Crystal Bowl White
Imperial Frosty Rose	and Yellow	Maxim Sunset	Imperial Frosty Rose
Imperial Purple and White	Maxim Orange		Imperial Pink Shades
Majestic Giants Blue Shade	Maxim Red		Imperial Purple and White
Majestic Giants White	Maxim Sunset		
Melody Light Blue	Padparadja		

color wheel. Mix red, orange, and purple for a showstopping arrangement. Or try blue, purple, and red for drama. Combine yellow, lime green, and orange for a bright display.

Repetition

When you combine plants in a pot, limit the number of different shapes or textures; otherwise your planting may lack definition. Repeat the same flower shape and size or leaf shape and size several times to create a harmonious mix and a soothing overall impression; then add something radically different for excitement. For example, punctuate a low mass of yellow pansies with tall white narcissus or plant some long fern fronds to enliven a large clump of white impatiens. Repeating the same color, texture, or plant in different containers also helps unify a grouping of pots.

Fragrance

To add extra mystery, enjoyment, and romance to the garden, choose plants with exotic or familiar scents, which arouse the emotions and are a powerful link to memory.

A container of lemon herbs on your patio will release a zesty fragrance during the heat of the day. Sweetly fragrant paperwhites can perfume a whole garden, while a summer-blooming gardenia delights those who are dining outdoors or just enjoying the night air in the garden. Place fragrant container gardens close to where you pass by during the day or relax in the evening. Or set them near a door or a window that is frequently open.

Small pots of sweet alyssum and Bethlehem narcissus emit a soft perfume.

Creating Classic Combinations

In containers, plants can be used singly or in combination. When deciding how many plants to use, consider the container. If the pot is elaborate in form or color, avoid upstaging it with a lush mixed planting. A plain container, on the other hand, is perfect for luxurious combinations of flowers and foliage. Suggestions for combining plants and containers follow.

Working with a Single Plant Per Pot

Using one kind of plant per pot is preferable in some circumstances. Trees and large shrubs, vines, herbs, or vegetables should be planted singly because they grow very large. Single plants can also make spectacular specimens. Such plants typically have special foliage, flowers, or architectural interest year-round. Specimen plants include topiary, handsome evergreens, sculptural trees such as Japanese

An evergreen shrub is an ideal choice for display as a single plant or in a pair. This shrub's green, geometric form is a perfect complement to the classic faux limestone pot.

maples, and striking shrubs such as yucca or palm. Essential to success with a single plant is to choose a container that complements the plant's size and texture.

Grouping Containers for Impact

A grouping of pots is unified by the same material (terra-cotta) and the same plant genre (succulents). A folk-art jug adds personality.

Grouping containers allows you to place several plants or pots together for interesting design options. Using a number of identical pots in a line gives the effect of a formal raised bed or a low wall. Clustering pots of different shapes and sizes but of the same color creates an informal garden with a theme. For a small grouping, try using three to five pots in a triangle. Unify a collection of dissimilar pots by repeating plants with the same color and texture and by using lush plantings and trailers.

Evergreens in Containers

In cooler climates, the choice of plants for winter display is limited. One solution is to use an evergreen shrub year-round and then add containers of flowers in the spring, the summer, and the fall. Evergreen shrubs are without question the most versatile shrubs in the landscape. Planting them in containers makes them even more useful. Natural sites for evergreens include by the front door, at the entry to the garden, or on a terrace that looks bare in the winter. Depending on what is cold hardy in your area, you can choose from a variety of evergreens, including arborvitae, boxwood, camellia, dwarf Alberta spruce, fatsia, holly, juniper, palm, pine, and yew. Evergreens also double as holiday decorations or gifts.

Large fronds of saw palmetto make a bold statement in this evergreen arrangement, underscored by the floppy leaves of foxglove, a quiet patch of Johnny-jump-ups, and trailing English ivy.

43

A mixture of geraniums, caladiums, petunias, and trailing fan flower and vinca, this arrangement has all the elements of a successful container garden: texture, height, form, and color.

Designing with Plants in Containers

When planting your containers, follow the same principles used when creating flower arrangements. Abundance and repetition are the keys to massing lots of one kind of plant—in one or two compatible colors—in one container. Massing works well in low, shallow containers, such as dishes, window boxes, and planter boxes. For example, try planting a mass of white and yellow daffodils, pink and purple petunias, or yellow and pale purple pansies.

When mixing different plants in one container, focus on contrasting the plants' textures, heights, forms, and colors. Vary the textures and the sizes of leaves or add a tall plant for height. To make the pot appear even fuller, use compact plants to create mass and trailing plants to soften edges of the pot and to spill over the container. Choose flowers and colorful foliage that contrast well.

PLANTS FOR MIXING

Here are some choices to consider when planning containers with mixed plants.

Foliage plants. Croton, dusty miller, fern, herbs, hosta, lamb's ears, lettuce, ornamental grasses, palms, sedum, shrubs, trees, and tropicals.

Plants with height. Daffodils, hosta, ornamental grasses, shrubs, topiary, trees, tropicals, and tulips.

Trailing plants. Bougainvillea, cotoneaster, fern, ivy, lantana, periwinkle, petunia, portulaca, prostrate rosemary, shore juniper, thyme, and verbena.

Plants with spiked foliage, such as dragon plant, add height and excitement to a container of achimenes.

Three Seasons of a Pot

Give your garden a quick seasonal update by making a container the focus of a particular planting scheme. Containers set in a flowerbed add height and serve as pedestals for plantings that need more emphasis.

The pot planted for all seasons (shown at right) serves a dual purpose: it anchors the corner of a rustic cedar arbor and gives low-growing annuals the height and the mass of a small shrub. When planning the color scheme of a pot that is to be set in a flowerbed, take into account the plantings that surround the container. The continuity between the bed and the pot creates a greater impact than does the dressed-up pot alone. Success depends on understanding the cycle of cool- and warm-weather plants and arranging plants creatively in the container. The container garden shown receives morning sunlight and afternoon shade.

Winter to spring

Winter to spring. A carpet of pink and rose pansies (top right) echoes the colors of foxgloves when they rise in the spring border. White sweet alyssum, which has bloomed off and on since the fall, now opens like a lace doily. Parsley grows with a flourish in the spring, although it has been present throughout the winter. The spring pot brims with an abundance of cool-weather plants that are repeated at the container's feet. Glacier English ivy gives the pot an established look and ties it into the surrounding garden.

Summer

Summer. In the summer, tiered plant forms and a harmony of foliage colors (center right) create a striking combination. Purple-leafed fountain grass provides the upright form, while the trailing ornamental Blackie sweet potato vine echoes the foliage color of the grass. A sunset-colored dwarf hibiscus fills the middle ground. This plant also supplies some flower color and links the pot with the coppery coleus at the base of the container and the melampodium in the bed.

Fall. The tawny hue of the Autumn Joy sedum in the background (bottom right) quietly echoes the brick red of chrysanthemums. The melampodium in the bed has grown more outstanding by the fall and influences the color scheme, which now includes golden marigolds and chartreuse Oak Leaf lettuce. Ornamental cabbage gives the planting the mass it needs to become an accent at the arbor-covered entrance to the autumn garden. In the fall, remaining warm-weather annuals, like this melampodium, coexist with fall-planted cool-weather plants, such as the lettuce and the ornamental cabbage, until the first frost.

Fall

Succulent

Plants for Year-round Beauty

Here are some good choices for seasonal offerings of flowers, foliage, and fragrance.

SPRING

Chives
Cilantro
Daffodil
Dianthus
Dill
Hyacinth
Jasmine
Little Gem magnolia
Meyer lemon
Ornamental cabbage and kale
Pansy
Petunia
Primrose
Rose
Ryegrass
Snapdragon
Star magnolia
Sweet alyssum
Tulip

Pansies

SUMMER

Banana	Hibiscus
Basil	Hosta
Bay	Impatiens
Bee balm	Lavender
Begonia	Lemon herbs
Bougainvillea	Madagascar periwinkle
Burnet	Mandevilla
Caladium	Marjoram
Catnip	Portulaca
Coleus	Rain lily
Crepe myrtle	Rose
Daylily	Rose verbena
Dusty miller	Scarlet sage
Fennel	Scented geranium
Fern	Spider lily
Feverfew	Succulents
Gardenia	Zinnia
Geranium	
Ginger lily	
Gladiolus	
Globe amaranth	

WINTER

Amaryllis
Artemisia
Boxwood
Common camellia
Common periwinkle
Crocus
Dwarf Alberta spruce
Dwarf mugho pine
English ivy
Germander
Hinoki false cypress
Japanese yew
Juniper
Lamb's ears
Leyland cypress
Little Gem magnolia
Mint
Nandina
Ornamental cabbage
  and kale
Pansy
Primrose
Pyracantha
Ribbon grass
River birch
Rosemary
Spruce pine
Sweet flag
Thyme

Common camellia

FALL

Aster
Chrysanthemum
Cotoneaster
Fountain grass
Japanese maple
Marigold
Melampodium
Mexican mint marigold
Narrow-leaf zinnia
Oregano
Pansy
Rose
Sage
Salvia
Sasanqua camellia
Sedum
Yaupon holly

Rose

Planting and Care

Planting container gardens is easy and fun, but remember that the plants depend on you to care for them.

Small hanging baskets are perfect for adding color and vertical interest, using only a few plants, such as these double impatiens.

Follow a few basic potting guidelines, and you can create a container garden in a weekend. Once you have finished planting, caring for your garden begins. Potted plants cannot take care of themselves the way plants in the ground can; plants in containers cannot compensate as easily for deficiencies in soil texture and fertility or for too much or too little rainfall. Your container plants will rely almost totally on you for care.

Planting in Containers

While there is nothing difficult about planting in containers, you will need to pay attention to the selection of potting soil, the containers, and the transplants that go in these.

No matter what you grow, always use quality potting soil. Garden soil is not well suited to the needs of plants in containers; it is too heavy, often does not drain well, and can harbor insects and diseases. Plants in containers need adequate moisture so that they do not dry out and excellent drainage so that their roots don't rot. The ideal potting mix is one that absorbs water quickly and also retains moisture without becoming waterlogged. In addition, it includes other special ingredients that are important to the success of your plants.

To create optimum growing conditions, choose your containers carefully. Remember that lightweight, easily moved pots are ideal for annuals, herbs, perennials, succulents, and seasonal spots of color. However, you need heavier large pots for vegetables, large tropicals, and permanent plantings of roses, shrubs, and trees. Just be sure to purchase plants that are healthy and appropriate for your needs.

Set your large containers where you intend to display them before you begin planting; the pots will be heavy and hard to move after they are filled.

Start with Quality Potting Mix

Always start with a premium commercial potting mix. Although potting mixes are usually called potting soil, they do not actually contain garden soil. Instead, they are artificial "soil" mixes, made of such ingredients as sphagnum peat moss, composted bark, vermiculite, perlite, and sand. However, not all mixes contain these quality ingredients, and the labels on some of the cheaper brands may not even indicate the contents. So how do you eliminate confusion and learn to recognize a good mix? Quality mixes are porous, are lightweight to medium-weight, drain well, and contain the ingredients previously mentioned. Deluxe mixes also contain lime to balance the pH; many may also include a controlled-release fertilizer and water-retaining polymers. While more expensive, these deluxe mixes are usually a better buy, especially if you are creating a permanent or perennial container garden.

Read the labels on the bags for mixes carefully. At first, buy small quantities of several mixes to sample them and to see which performs best for your plants. Avoid inexpensive mixes that do not list ingredients. And do not choose special fine-textured mixes that are meant to be used for starting plants from seed; these are too lightweight and pack down too easily to be used for full-sized plants.

A quality potting mix is essential for growing plants in containers successfully.

A POTTING SOIL RECIPE

If you have many large pots to fill, it may be more economical to mix your own potting soil. Here is a recipe for a general mix. For growing large shrubs and trees, replace peat moss with more composted bark (or even bagged topsoil) for moisture retention and weight.

Use a 3-gallon bucket to fill a 3-cubic-foot wheelbarrow with:

1 bucket sphagnum peat moss
1 bucket coarse builder's sand
1 bucket finely ground bark
    (often sold as soil conditioner)
2 cups lime
⅓ pound iron sulfate
2 pounds controlled-release
    flower food or 6 pounds
    cottonseed meal

Use your shovel to blend the ingredients in a wheelbarrow. Stir well to ensure that the soil is evenly mixed. Gently dampen the mixture with a sprinkler, stopping every few minutes to turn the soil thoroughly. When the mix is moist (not soggy), it is ready to use. Store any leftover soil in a large plastic garbage can with a sealed lid.

Some gardeners recommend modifying a basic all-purpose potting mix for plants with special needs. For example, if you are planting trees, shrubs, roses, and tropicals, add extra sand and compost to a basic mix to increase the container's weight and to balance the top growth of larger plants. The sand also improves porosity and drainage. Also for these same plants, blend in extra composted pine bark to improve moisture retention. Always remember that the properties of potting mix are affected by the size and the shape of the container. The taller the container, for example, the better the drainage, because water drains to the bottom of the pot. Smaller, shallower containers may not drain through as well, but they tend to lose moisture through evaporation.

Controlled-release fertilizer. A controlled-release fertilizer is one of several additives that you will find in a quality potting soil mix. However, most potting soils don't contain enough fertilizer to make a big difference in plant growth, so you'll need to add more. Nutrients in controlled-release fertilizer are coated and are released gradually over several weeks or months, depending on the soil moisture or temperature. Controlled-release fertilizer is ideal for the busy gardener, because it does not have to be applied often. There are many brands available that are effective for two to nine months at soil temperatures of around 70 degrees. However, in containers that are watered often in the summer, it may not last quite as long. Flowers often need extra soluble fertilizer every couple of weeks during the peak blooming season.

The label on the bag will indicate whether a fertilizer contains controlled-release nitrogen. This element is necessary for healthy plant growth. Only purchase a fertilizer that contains 30 to 50 percent controlled-release nitrogen.

Water-retaining polymers. Another addition that simplifies the maintenance of plants in containers is water-retaining polymers, which soak up many times their weight in water and hold the water in reserve so that it is available to plants as they need it. Polymers help reduce the chance of overwatering (which causes plants to rot) or underwatering (which causes drought stress in container plants). Polymer material comes in a crystal-like form that resembles rock salt. It should be soaked in water and mixed with the potting soil before planting. (Some soil mixes already have polymers added.) Polymers are especially useful in small containers, such as window boxes, hanging baskets, and shallow dishes, which dry out quickly in hot summer sunlight.

Select Appropriate Pots

One of the most common mistakes gardeners make is cramming a large plant into a small pot. The plant should be comfortable in its pot. The larger the pot, the better the drainage, the insulation, and the simulation of real garden conditions. Take a ruler or a tape measure with you to the garden shop when you need to buy a pot. Choose a pot that allows at least 1 to 2 inches between the root ball of the plant and the side of the container. If you are mixing a number of transplants that have tiny root balls no larger than individual cells in a cell pack, space the plants at least one-half the recommended spacing and 2 to 3 inches from the rim of the pot.

Cachepots. If you have a decorative container that you want to use outdoors, try the double-potting approach. Leave your chosen plant in a plastic nursery pot or replant it in any attractive pot that has drainage holes. Place the planted pot inside the decorative pot (which has drainage holes as well). When cold weather comes, bring the plant with its two pots indoors and set a saucer underneath. This works well with clay-colored plastic and clay pots.

You can also leave a cachepot in place to display a series of seasonal plants in their original nursery pots. For example, a colorful collection of primroses can be followed by a mix of tulips and daffodils; replace these first with an azalea, and then marigolds, and finally mums.

Saucers and feet. A saucer catches the water that drains out of the pot and protects the surface on which the pot is sitting. Be careful not to overwater so that the saucer is always full and the plant stands in water, as this can promote root rot. You may want to remove saucers temporarily during prolonged periods of rain.

Clay feet placed under a pot aid in drainage, preventing the pot from sitting in water. Keeping the base of the pot out of water helps slow the chipping and cracking process that clay containers undergo during cold months. Stones and bricks can serve as feet, or you may want to use clay or concrete animal paws that are reminiscent of the feet on Victorian furniture. These will protect your deck surface better than will a brick.

Planting and Potting

Buy transplants that are green, firm, and healthy looking; avoid those that are lanky, overgrown, or yellowing. If a transplant's roots are creamy white, the plant is healthy; if they are brown and matted, the plant is root bound and will not get off to a good start. If you want a

Shrubs such as this pittosporum can develop extensive roots and need a pot large enough to accommodate their growth.

Healthy transplants have a network of strong white roots.

An ordinary paper coffee filter placed over the drainage hole of a pot will let water drain out but will keep the potting soil in.

When combining plants, be sure they are horticulturally compatible. These tulips and hyacinths require sun and excellent drainage.

particular color of flower, select the plant when it's in bloom. To envision how certain plants will work together, move them around and group them right there at the garden shop. That way, you will have a better idea of which plants to buy.

Planting single large plants. For plants with root balls that are 1-gallon size or larger, select a pot that is 3 to 5 inches wider in diameter than the root ball (or the nursery pot). Cover the drainage hole in the new pot with gravel, screening, broken pieces of clay pot, or a coffee filter to keep the potting medium from washing out of the hole when you water. Add enough moistened potting mix so that the plant's root ball sits up to within 2 inches of the top of the container.

Gently remove the plant from its container and place it in the new pot. If the plant's root ball appears compacted, cut it vertically with a knife, and spread out the roots. Fill in spaces around the side with moistened potting mix, packing it lightly so that the top of the root ball is level with the mix and within 2 inches of the top of the container. Do not fill the pot too full, or the soil will wash out during watering. Also, do not set plants too high (a common mistake in container gardening). With annuals and bulbs, set transplants in a pot at half the spacing recommended for the garden. With all other plants, allow for regular spacing. Water thoroughly and gently.

If you are planting a heavy shrub or tree, place 2 to 3 inches of gravel in the bottom of the pot to add weight; this will keep it from tipping over in the wind.

Mixing plants in containers. When choosing plants to mix in the same container, make sure they are similar in light, moisture, and fertilizer requirements, as well as in size and growth habits. For example, some plants—such as fern, caladium, and impatiens—need shade and have high moisture requirements; these plants can be combined in the same container. Other plants, such as sedum, portulaca, and yucca, are sun loving and drought tolerant; group them together.

If you are not aware of a particular plant's growing requirements, you could have problems when it is combined with another plant in a container. For example, if you mix a caladium with a portulaca, you will probably kill one or the other plant. The caladium will both shade the sun-loving annual and suffer in the heat. And if you give the caladium the water it requires to thrive, the portulaca will probably rot.

Caring for Your Plants

Good container gardening habits are necessary for success with your plants. Be aware of seasonal changes and what ongoing care is necessary. Just as when they are in the garden, plants need water and mulch to keep their roots cool and moist and fertilizer to supply energy.

Cool Weather Versus Warm Weather

Container gardeners need to know how seasonal rhythms affect plants in containers. During *cool weather*—late fall through early spring—container gardens receive lots of rain and have few pests. The chief concern is the cold; the roots of plants in containers are exposed to more cold than are the roots of plants in the ground. Pots and plants may need protection from wind and cold. When the temperature drops to just 10 degrees above the normal hardiness range for the plants that you are growing, you may wish to move the plants to a sheltered niche. Consider doing so especially if the drop is sudden and was preceded by mild weather; plants will not have had a chance to *harden off* (get accustomed to cooler weather), thus making them susceptible to cold damage. If you wish to leave the plants in place, mound materials such as pine straw or evergreen boughs (perhaps from a Christmas tree) around and over the pot.

In *warm weather*—late spring through late fall—plants in containers are more likely to suffer from dehydration and excessive heat and are more likely to have insect and disease problems (which are at their peak in the summer). At this time, plants may use water faster than nature replaces it. Containers, particularly those in full sunlight, should be checked almost daily to ensure that its soil is adequately moist. It helps to apply a layer of organic mulch, such as pine bark, or a decorative stone mulch to the top of the potting mix; mulch retains moisture and insulates the mix from the heat.

Watering

Get in the habit of testing for soil moisture whenever you walk past your containers. Poke your index finger into the pot to a depth of 1 inch; if the potting mix feels dry, it is time to water. Do not let the potting mix completely dry out, or the soil will separate from the pot and the water will run down the outside edge of the soil when you water and will not reach the plant's roots.

These pots of lettuce and marigolds require the same amount of attention as do plants in the ground.

During the summer, you need to water container plants in full sunlight, such as these petunias, almost every day.

Basil and garlic chives flourish in this self-watering container, which is ideal for busy gardeners.

To make watering convenient, keep a hose and a watering can nearby. You may even want to set up a drip system, connected to an outdoor spigot, to do the work for you. These systems supply a slow, steady trickle of moisture and can be regulated by an automatic timer that turns the flow on and off at programmed hours. You can conceal drip attachments in the soil and at the back of the pot. Drip irrigation is particularly useful for large expensive trees and shrubs. Self-watering containers, or containers with reservoirs at the bottom, are also a convenient way to keep plants moist.

If you are leaving for a week's vacation in the summer, take the time to set your plants in a large plastic wading pool located in the shade. Then water the plants thoroughly and fill the pool with 1 inch of water. The pool will act as a large saucer and will water plants from the bottom until you return.

A child's wading pool is ideal for keeping containers moist while you are on vacation.

Mulching the soil in the container will prevent water loss through evaporation, but, just as importantly, mulch is also part of the container design. Spanish moss lights up the base of the planting, contrasts with dark containers, and has an attractive texture. Pinecones complement cinnamon-colored bark or echo the richness of flowers and foliage. Pine bark nuggets or shredded bark have a somewhat coarse texture that visually supports designs featuring large-leafed plants. Soil conditioner (finely ground pine bark) is the best material for designs that include annuals or herbaceous perennials because the fineness of the material complements the plants.

THIRSTY PLANTS

These plants require frequent watering—sometimes every day during the warm season.

- Moisture-loving plants, such as impatiens, hosta, and azaleas

- Vegetables and fruits

- Plants in full sunlight

- Plants in shallow containers, which allow a lot of moisture to evaporate

- Trees and shrubs that have been in containers for several years, because they probably are root-bound

Fertilizing

Constant watering leaches fertilizer from the soil, so you need to fertilize plants in containers regularly. When planting, incorporate a controlled-release fertilizer into the soil. Fertilize according to package instructions for the specific plants you are growing. About two to three months after planting, scratch controlled-release fertilizer into the surface of the soil, using a hard tool such as a small trowel. Because potted plants require such frequent watering, count on a controlled-release fertilizer to be effective only one-half to two-thirds of the time specified on its label. A supplemental feeding of water-soluble 20–20–20 or 15–30–15 fertilizer (these numbers are explained in the next paragraph) applied throughout the growing season should be sufficient. You may need to apply it every two weeks for flowering plants, but only monthly for trees and shrubs. Use label directions as the final guide.

A fertilizer is labeled with a number stating the percentage of the three major nutrients it contains. The first number represents nitrogen (N), which stimulates foliage growth. The second number represents phosphorus (P), which promotes root growth and flowering. The last number represents potassium (K), which enhances cold hardiness, disease resistance, and all-around plant health. You may wish to use a bloom booster with a higher middle number, such as 15–30–15, to get more prolific blooms on your annuals or perennials.

Feed your flowers with a bloom booster to stimulate blossoms. In the winter, a product that contains mostly nitrate nitrogen is better for pansies and other cool-weather flowers because it is available in cool soils.

Maintaining Healthy Plants

It is as important to maintain healthy plants as it is to get them started out correctly. Learn when each one needs repotting, pruning, and deadheading and which ones can be overwintered successfully. Once you understand and meet your plants' needs, they will reward you with year-round color and foliage.

Repotting

In humid climates, the organic material in a soil mix will decompose within a year, causing the mix to lose its texture and to become compacted. In cold climates, the soil mix may last two years. Depending on where you live, you need to replace the potting soil annually or every other year. Repotting a plant the proper way will not disturb its root ball and, thus, can be done practically at any time. However, you may wish to avoid repotting during the hottest months of the summer, so as not to disturb the roots during periods of stress.

Annuals and vegetables are not repotted. Simply start fresh each year with new soil mix. Use the old potting soil as an amendment in your garden soil or add it to the compost pile.

In the case of small perennial plantings, such as herbs, ferns, grasses, and bulbs, repotting is easy. Gently remove the plant from its old container and follow the suggestions for potting as discussed on pages 51 and 52.

Repotting large trees, shrubs, and tropicals is a little more involved. Repot as you would a small perennial, until the plant and the pot reach the maximum allowable size for the site; from then on you must repot while the plant is dormant, typically in the winter or in early spring. Carefully lay the plant on its side and pull off the pot, taking care not to yank the central stem and perhaps detach it from the roots. Trim some of the old root tips but remove no more than 25 percent of the roots. Then repot the plant in the same container, using new potting mix.

Pruning and Deadheading

Pruning is essential to healthy plant growth and to the maintenance of a tidy shape in the case of roses, shrubs, and trees. As a general rule, prune no more than one-third of the plant at a time, while following the plant's natural form. Take out dead wood and crisscrossing branches first. Prune spring-blooming shrubs immediately *after* they have stopped flowering because they will bloom next year on this new growth. Prune summer-blooming shrubs in late winter or early spring *before* new growth begins because they will bloom this summer on the new growth.

Some annuals and herbs also benefit from pruning. When blooming begins to slow, pinch back lanky annuals, such as petunias and scarlet sage, to promote production of side shoots and additional blossoms. Regularly snip the stems of herbs, especially annual and biennial herbs grown for foliage, such as basil, cilantro, dill, parsley, and summer savory. This keeps plants bushy and productive, prolonging the harvesting season.

Deadheading (snipping back spent blossoms) is also key for growing healthy, productive plants. Do not let the spent blossoms go to seed, as this uses up vital energy that the plant could put into blooming. Regularly deadhead annuals, perennials, and bulbs. A few annual herbs grown for foliage, such as basil and cilantro, require deadheading so that they do not bolt or go to seed too early.

Keep petunias in bloom by regularly removing blossoms as they fade.

Staking can be as charming as it is practical. Here, a ring of grapevine keeps a planting of paperwhites standing tall.

Staking

Such plants as tall bulbs, perennials, and tomatoes need to be staked for support. Insert the stake into the container when you plant, pushing it down until it hits the bottom of the pot. Tie the plant to the stake as it grows, using loose twine or fabric that will not harm the stems. You can use stakes in an ornamental way, choosing from the variety of wrought iron, bamboo, copper, and other staking products available in garden shops and catalogues.

Overwintering

Be prepared to overwinter tender tropicals, herbs, succulents, or prized annuals or perennials that you wish to propagate. Plants can be overwintered in one of two ways, depending on the size of the plant and the kind of indoor space that you have to offer. Store plants in the house, in a heated garage, or in front of a sunny window at least 1 foot away from the windowpane (to protect against cold air that permeates the glass). Plants may continue to grow and even flower under these circumstances. If they do, feed and water them regularly. Or you can move the plants to a cool, dark basement or garage, where they will go dormant. In this case, do not fertilize plants and only water very sparingly, letting the soil dry between waterings. Cut the plants back if you wish to make them easier to keep. Many will drop their leaves anyway and need some cutting back when you put them out again in spring.

In areas where gardenias freeze if left outdoors, grow them in containers and overwinter in a sunny location indoors.

Container plants are more vulnerable to cold than are garden plants because the potting mix in containers freezes and thaws faster than the ground. In particular, potting soil in hanging baskets, window boxes, and other raised pots freezes faster than does mix in containers placed on the ground.

Here are some ways to protect plant roots.

- Water plants before a heavy freeze.

- Move plants to a protected south-facing niche.

- Mound bales of pine straw around the feet of the container.

- Adorn plants with small white Christmas lights, which can sometimes provide enough heat to get the plants through the worst of the winter.

Plant Hardiness Zone Map

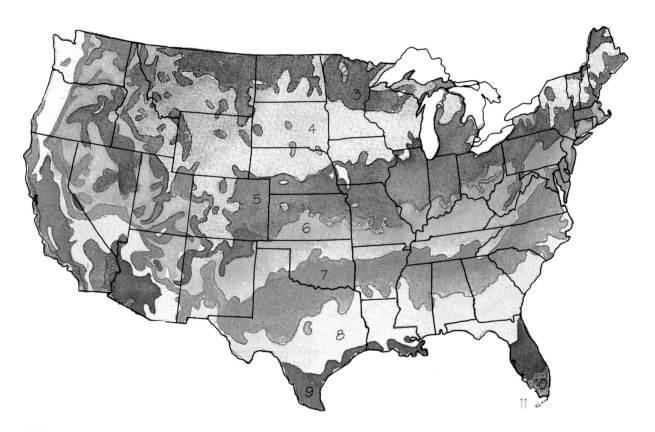

The United States Department of Agriculture (USDA) has charted low temperatures throughout the country to determine the ranges of average low readings. The map above is based loosely on the USDA Plant Hardiness Zone Map, which was drawn from these findings. It does not take into account heat, soil, or moisture extremes and is intended as a guide, not as a guarantee.

The southern regions of the United States that are mentioned in this book refer to the following:

Upper South: Zone 6

Middle South: upper region of Zone 7 (0 to 5 degrees minimum)

Lower South: lower region of Zone 7 and upper region of Zone 8 (5 to 15 degrees minimum)

Coastal South: lower region of Zone 8 and upper region of Zone 9 (15 to 25 degrees minimum)

Tropical South: lower region of Zone 9 and all of Zone 10 (25 to 40 degrees minimum)

Zone 2	-50	to	-40°F
Zone 3	-40	to	-30°F
Zone 4	-30	to	-20°F
Zone 5	-20	to	-10°F
Zone 6	-10	to	0°F
Zone 7	0	to	10°F
Zone 8	10	to	20°F
Zone 9	20	to	30°F
Zone 10	30	to	40°F
Zone 11		above	40°F

Plant Profiles

The following chapters focus on specific groups of plants that flourish in containers. Use the photographs to get more ideas for placing and combining annuals and perennials, bulbs, herbs and vegetables, trees and shrubs, roses, and tropicals.

The charts in each chapter profile a few of the best species and selections for containers. However, do not limit your choices to these as literally hundreds of plants are suitable for container gardening. Plants are listed alphabetically by common **Name,** followed by the botanical name (genus and species) in italic, plus additional species or selections and types. Roses are an exception. Because they are all of the *Rosa* species, the entries are by selection only, followed by type of rose.

Drought-tolerant purslane is a good choice for a summer container plant.

Each plant profile includes **Features** (a brief description), **Light** and **Water** requirements, **Range** (zones of hardiness), and **Comments** (additional planting information). **Season** indicates the time of peak interest (foliage, color, blooms, or bark) for flowers, trees, shrubs, and tropicals. In the herb and vegetable charts, the season of growth and harvest is designated. Those that grow in the fall, the winter, or early spring are called cool-weather vegetables or herbs; those that prefer summer are warm-weather vegetables.

Natural Size in every chart indicates the size that a plant reaches in the landscape. A tree or shrub obviously is dwarfed by being in a pot and grows only as large as its root system can support. The larger the container, the larger the plant will grow. Most annuals, perennials, herbs, and vegetables are likely to grow to near their natural size if the pot is big enough to allow this; therefore, their width is also given. Width is not a factor with vining plants or roses.

Possible **Pests** are given for all plants except bulbs, where the entry is replaced with **Planting Tips.** Spacing of bulbs at planting is critical to success, and bulbs rarely are infested with pests. Following the Plant Profiles is a section on the insects that may attack your plants in containers and the diseases that can affect these plants.

Annuals and Perennials

Potted flowers, such as geraniums, pansies, petunias, and sedum, transform a set of plain brick steps into a miniature garden.

The most colorful and varied groups of plants for pots, annuals and perennials require careful selection.

Fill containers with annuals and perennials and place the pots strategically for a succession of colorful flowers in an otherwise all-green garden. Whether used alone or mixed, potted annuals and perennials provide long-lasting color in the landscape. The key is to choose the right plants for the season and to keep them watered, fertilized, and deadheaded, if needed.

Choosing Annuals for Containers

Annuals are the most popular flowering plants to grow in containers. Inexpensive and readily available, they are ideal for gardeners who want to change plants seasonally or for a special event, such as a party. Annuals grow, bloom, and set seed in one year or less; then they are killed by frost or extreme heat. The advantage is that annuals may last four to eight months, which allows them to create maximum impact in the garden.

While containerized trees and shrubs are relatively permanent features in the landscape, potted annuals are strictly temporary. If a plant doesn't live up to your expectations or does not perform well, simply replace it. Use annuals in containers to enhance the garden in many ways. For example, place a collection of spring-blooming plants, such as pansies, sweet alyssum, and old-fashioned petunias, near a walkway, a bench, or a window to add both color and scent to the garden. Set a plant that hummingbirds love, such as impatiens, in a hanging basket near a feeder to attract these birds during their spring or fall migration.

Purchasing Annuals

When buying annuals, first select a plant for sun or shade, depending on what your location offers. Remember, almost all annuals appreciate some shade when there is hot afternoon sun. Placing pots where the shadow of a nearby tree or a roofline falls in late afternoon prevents wilting in hot sunlight. If you want to be sure of the color of your flowers, look for plants that are in bloom.

Cool-Weather and Warm-Weather Annuals

All annuals are divided into two groups, according to when they grow—cool weather (late fall, winter, and early spring) and warm weather (late spring, summer, and early fall). Generally, plants are only available during their prime season, but it will help you to know which plants do best in which seasons so that you don't buy them at the end of a cycle. Warm-weather annuals include coleus, impatiens, Madagascar periwinkle, marigolds, verbena, and wax begonias. Among the best choices for shade are impatiens and coleus; wax begonias thrive in partial shade. See the charts beginning on page 66 for a guide to the season of bloom for many annuals often grown in containers.

In colder regions of the South, the choice of cool-weather annual flowers is limited to the most hardy pansies. One way to keep color in the winter is to use a hardy grass, such as rye, or an evergreen shrub, such as dwarf Alberta spruce, Japanese andromeda, Japanese yew, or juniper, in the center of the planting and to add pansies for the fall. You can later replace the pansies with warm-weather flowers.

Petunias flourish in a sunny window box from the spring through the fall. Variegated periwinkle, an evergreen vine, accentuates the draping effect.

The repetition of green and terra-cotta unifies this fall planting of annual rye.

61

Choosing Perennials for Containers

Perennials are less often grown in containers, because they have a shorter bloom time than do annuals—usually four to six weeks—and may die back completely in the off-season. Nevertheless, perennials are winning converts because of their stunning flowers, attractive foliage, and seasonal variety. Compared to annuals, which thrive for a single season, perennials can be more permanent additions to a container garden, lasting for several years. Also, since perennials tend to be more expensive than annuals, growing them in a container is a great way to try out one plant to see if you like it.

Because of the wide variety in size, shape, and form, not all perennials flourish in containers. For best results, see those listed in the chart beginning on page 68. The key to success with these plants is understanding their seasonal strengths. Some flowering perennials, such as rose verbena, coreopsis, and certain selections of daylily, bloom off and on all summer. Others, such as aster and chrysanthemum, put on a fabulous show for a month or two. Foliage plants, such as fountain grass, hosta, and ribbon grass, provide 8 to 12 months of color and texture. Take into account the particular characteristics of your perennials, and you will be able to enjoy the plants for many years.

The tops of most perennials are killed back by cold or go dormant in summer heat, but the roots survive and the stems will sprout again the next year. Because perennials undergo a dormant stage, growing them

Some perennials, such as rose verbena, provide a show of color all summer.

Planted in an attractive concrete pot, a simple evergreen, such as sweet flag, offers year-round color and texture in the Middle and Lower South.

A long-blooming yellow coreopsis and a fall-blooming purple aster are paired to extend the season of color.

in containers requires planning. You must either mix perennials with annuals to cover up faded foliage or change containers planted only with perennials as soon as the plants begin to lose their charm. Use evergreen perennials, such as sweet flag, Bath's Pink dianthus, lamb's ears, and liriope in combination with flowering annuals or perennials to anchor a planting and to carry it through the off-season. Ivy and common periwinkle have the added feature of being vining plants, which cascade over the sides of containers for a lush effect.

Choosing Containers for Annuals and Perennials

Shallow-rooted annuals are perfect candidates for dishes, hanging baskets, and window boxes. They also work well in unusual pots or converted treasures, such as small wagons, watering cans, or fruit crates. Long-lived perennials, which have more extensive root systems, require deeper pots and more soil than do many annuals. When in doubt, pick a pot that is larger than you think is needed.

Perennials that spend the winter outside must be planted in pots that withstand freezing weather. Terra-cotta pots crumble in areas that have freezing winter temperatures. You may wish to grow

Most perennials, such as these asters, need larger, deeper pots than do annuals, because of their taproots.

perennials in pots fitted inside second pots so that the plants can be replaced with others when they reach their off-season.

Containerized annuals and perennials are susceptible to drying out in the summer if they are placed in direct sunlight. For summer plantings in full sunlight, some gardeners prefer plastic or foam pots, which don't dry out as quickly. Others slip the containers into cachepots. Putting a pot inside a larger container also helps insulate the roots from the heat of the sun. Exceptions are grasses, Mediterranean herbs, and succulents, which can dry out slightly between waterings. (See pages 24–33 for more information on choosing containers.)

Get to know the differences between annuals and perennials, as well as how they are often described.

Annual: A herbaceous plant that sprouts, blooms, produces seed, and dies within a year.

Cool-weather annual: One that is planted in the fall or early spring and blooms through the cool months until high summer temperatures cause the plant to deteriorate or cease blooming.

Warm-weather annual: One that is planted in late spring, after the threat of frost has passed, and blooms throughout the summer and early fall, until killed by frost.

Perennial: A plant whose foliage, and usually stems, are killed by winter cold or summer heat but whose roots survive, causing it to return each year. A few perennials are evergreen, so they don't die back. Examples include Lenten rose and liriope.

Hardy: An annual or perennial capable of withstanding freezing temperatures in the winter.

Half-hardy: An annual or perennial that can survive mild winters.

Evergreen: A plant that keeps its foliage and color year-round.

Flowers such as these petunias and geraniums need a quality potting soil to thrive in containers.

Plants in 4-inch pots or larger will make a window box look full from the beginning.

Planting Annuals and Perennials in Containers

Annuals and perennials are usually planted early in the fall, spring, or summer, depending on the type of plant, its seasonal show, and its winter hardiness. Generally, plant cool-weather annuals and hardy spring-blooming perennials in early fall; hardy summer- and fall-blooming perennials in early spring; and warm-weather annuals and tender perennials in late spring or summer, after the threat of frost has passed. If you want instant color, start with large plants, as they provide a show more quickly than do smaller plants. One trick is to purchase nearly full-size plants in a hanging basket; remove them from the basket and then transplant them to a sizable patio pot. Occasionally, you may also find large annuals grown in 1– to 3–gallon containers.

Potting Soil

In general, flowers prefer a fluffy, lightweight soil mix that will hold plenty of moisture but will not get too soggy. The labels on some bagged soils indicate that the soils are geared specifically for certain types of plants, such as flowers. A quality all-purpose potting soil that contains similar proportions of ingredients is also adequate. You will need to read labels carefully to make a decision. Avoid sandy soils, such as those for cacti and succulents, because they dry out too quickly. To keep plants moist during hot weather, use a soil that contains a wetting agent and a water-retaining polymer. (See pages 49 and 50 for more information about potting soils.)

How to Plant

A pot filled with soil is often heavy, so be sure to place a container where you plan to display it before starting to plant. To prepare the pot, cover the drainage hole with coarse screen so that the soil does not wash out. Add moistened potting mix until the pot is almost full, leaving enough room for the root balls of the chosen transplants. Mix a controlled-release fertilizer into the potting mix.

To place transplants, gently slide the container from the plant, being careful not to pull the plant by its stem. Annual bedding and perennial plants often sit in garden centers for several weeks and are root bound by the time they are purchased, so be sure to tease roots apart before planting. If roots are heavily matted, make a cut in the bottom of the root ball and carefully pull the roots apart.

Place the plant in the new pot, with the surface of the root ball within 2 inches of the rim of the container. Fill in spaces around the sides with moistened potting mix, firming the surface with your fingers. Level off the mix even with the top of the root ball. Do not fill the pot too full, or the soil will wash out when you water. Leave at least ½ to 1 inch of the pot's rim above the soil level. Be careful not to set the plant too high in the pot (a common mistake in container gardening), or the root ball will be exposed to air and will dry out. After planting, water the plant thoroughly. When planting annuals and perennials together, remember that annuals will be cut out after one season and perennials may remain in the pot for several years. To make replanting easier, set perennials in the back or the center of the container and plant annuals around the perimeter.

Care and Maintenance

Watering is the most critical part of maintenance for containerized annuals and perennials. Get in the habit of checking your plants regularly—daily, if they are in direct sunlight in the summer. To determine when to water, place your index finger into the potting mix; if the mix is dry to a depth of 1 inch, you need to water. Always water plants thoroughly to promote root growth. Pay particular attention to plants with high moisture requirements, such as coleus, ferns, hosta, impatiens, and periwinkle that quickly become root bound. If you do not have a lot of time to water plants in the summer, choose drought-tolerant plants, such as fountain grass, geranium, portulaca, and sedum.

Both annuals and perennials require regular fertilization. If you added a controlled-release fertilizer at planting, sprinkle more fertilizer into the soil surface after three months or when the label directions suggest. Supplement with a liquid fertilizer; use a bloom booster for flowering plants. (See page 55 for details on fertilizing.) In late summer, cut back on the feeding of those perennials that become dormant in the winter.

During the growing season, deadhead both annuals and perennials to remove spent blooms and to promote continued flowering. In the fall, cut back dead branches and foliage from perennials. If a perennial is the only plant in your container, move the pot to a less conspicuous spot in the garden for the off-season or replace the plant with different flowers. An additional option is to transplant the perennial into the garden for future seasons.

If properly fed and watered, annuals such as petunias and perennials such as variegated English ivy will grow rapidly, taking on an established look within a month.

ANNUALS

NAME/ SELECTIONS	FEATURES	SEASON	NATURAL SIZE	LIGHT	WATER	RANGE	PESTS/ DISEASES	COMMENTS
Coleus *Coleus hybridus* Burgundy Sun, Carefree, Plum Parfait, Wizard	Striking colorful foliage plant from chartreuse to burgundy to multicolored; Victorian style	Warm weather	6 inches to 3 feet tall, 6 to 12 inches wide	Full sun to shade	High	All zones	Whiteflies	Start from transplants in spring, 4 weeks after last frost; pinch flowers to keep plants bushy
Dusty Miller *Senecio cineraria* Cirrus, Silver Dust, Silver Queen	Woolly, old-fashioned plant prized for its silvery foliage; shrubby, tough; tolerates drought and freezing	Cool and warm weather	6 inches to 2 feet tall, 6 to 12 inches wide	Full sun to light shade	Low to medium	All zones; perennial in Zones 8 and 9	None specific	Start from transplants in early spring or early fall; remove flowers, cut back leggy plants
Geranium *Pelargonium* x *hortorum* Freckles, Orbit, Pinto Americana	Cottage garden plant with velvety leaves; white, pink, salmon, lavender, and red flowers	Cool and warm weather; blooms spring, summer, and fall	1 to 2 feet tall, equally wide	Full sun to partial shade; afternoon shade in summer	Low to medium	All zones	Whiteflies	Start from transplants in midspring; deadhead spent blooms; stimulate flowering with bloom-booster fertilizer
Globe Amaranth *Gomphrena globosa* Buddy, Dwarf White, Gnome	Charming plant with cloverlike blooms in white, pink, lavender, orange, red, or purple; attracts butterflies	Warm weather	8 inches to 2 feet tall, 8 to 12 inches wide	Full sun	Low to medium	All zones	None specific	Start from transplants in spring, 2 weeks after last frost; tough and long lasting; flowers dry well
Impatiens *Impatiens wallerana* Blitz, Elfin, New Guinea hybrids, Ripples, Twinkle	Nonstop blooms from spring until frost in lipstick colors; summer shade classic; attracts butterflies and hummingbirds	Warm weather	6 to 18 inches tall, 6 to 12 inches wide	Partial to full shade	High	All zones	None specific	Start from transplants in spring, 2 weeks after last frost; water well; cut back leggy plants to rejuvenate
Lantana *Lantana species* Dazzler, Lemon Swirl, Miss Huff, Pink Caprice, Radiation, Trailing Lantana	Tropical shrub with clusters of yellow, rose, lavender, and orange flowers; attracts butterflies; good for hanging baskets	Warm weather	1 to 2 feet tall, equally wide	Full sun	Low to medium	All zones; perennial in Zones 8 to 10	Spider mites, whiteflies	Start from transplants in spring, 2 weeks after last frost; long-blooming
Madagascar Periwinkle *Catharanthus roseus* Cooler Series, Little Series, Pacifica Series	Dependable phloxlike blooms for hot, dry weather in white, pink, lavender, rose, and red	Warm weather	3 to 15 inches tall, 3 to 6 inches wide	Full sun to partial shade	Low to medium	All zones	Root rot	Start from transplants in late spring, 1 month after last frost; do not set out too early
Marigold *Tagetes* hybrids FRENCH: Aurora, Bonanza, Hero, Janie, Sophia SIGNET: Golden Gem, Lemon Gem TRIPLOID: Fireworks, Solar, Sundance	Sunset-colored flowers for summer and fall; pungent ferny foliage; attracts butterflies; edible flowers used as garnish	Warm weather	6 to 18 inches tall, 6 to 10 inches wide	Full sun	Medium	All zones	Root rot, spider mites	Start from transplants in spring, 2 weeks after last frost; deadhead; cut back midseason to promote fall flowering or replace

ANNUALS

NAME/ SELECTIONS	FEATURES	SEASON	NATURAL SIZE	LIGHT	WATER	RANGE	PESTS/ DISEASES	COMMENTS
Melampodium *Melampodium paludosum* Medallion, Showstar	Mounding annual with bright green leaves covered with small, golden yellow daisies; good for hanging baskets	Warm weather	1½ to 2 feet tall, equally wide	Full sun to partial shade; blooms best in sun	Medium	All zones	None specific	Start in spring, 2 weeks after last frost; tough, tolerates heat and humidity; do not overfertilize; reseeds easily
Narrow-leaf Zinnia *Zinnia angustifolia* Classic Golden Orange, Crystal, White Star	Billowy plant with small, daisylike blooms until frost; flowers in orange and creamy white; good for hanging baskets	Warm weather	1 foot tall, equally wide	Full sun	Medium	All zones	None specific	Start in spring, 2 weeks after last frost; looks like a wildflower; low maintenance; heavy flowering
Ornamental Cabbage and Kale *Brassica oleracea* var. *acephala* Osaka Series	Leafy, bright rosettes in fall and winter; low-growing; foliage is green with white to red centers	Cool weather	6 to 10 inches tall, equally wide	Full sun	Medium	All zones	Cabbage-worms	Start from transplants in fall, 1 month before first frost; pull up in spring when heads grow tall
Pansy *Viola* x *Wittrockiana* Bingo, Crystal Bowl, Imperial Sky, Universal	Old-fashioned cottage flowers prized for color in fall, winter, and spring; blooms in white, orange, yellow, rose, blue, purple, and mixed colors	Cool weather	6 to 10 inches tall, 4 to 8 inches wide	Full sun	Medium	All zones	None specific	Start from transplants in fall, before first frost; feed with nitrate-based fertilizer to promote flowering
Petunia *Petunia* hybrids Celebrity Series, Fantasy Series, Madness Series, Wave Series	Bright summer color with blooms in purple, white, red, pink, blue, and mixed colors; attracts humming-birds; good for hang-ing baskets	Cool and warm weather	4 to 18 inches tall, 8 inches to 2 feet wide	Full sun to light shade	Low to medium	All zones	Root rot	Set out as transplants in early spring or late summer for fall; pinch back established plants for compact growth; old-fashioned types reseed
Portulaca *Portulaca species* and hybrids **Purslane** (*P. oleracea*)	Creeping succulents with colorful summer blooms in yellow, white, pink, red, pur-ple, and salmon; good for hanging baskets	Warm weather	4 to 8 inches tall, 6 to 18 inches wide	Full sun	Low to medium	All zones	None specific	Start with transplants in late spring, after last frost; keep plants full in center by cut-ting a few branches back every month
Primrose *Primula species*	Low-growing rosettes sporting gem-colored flowers; good for win-dow boxes in early spring	Cool weather	6 to 12 inches tall, 6 to 8 inches wide	Light shade	Medium to high	All zones	None specific	Start with transplants in late winter or early spring
Ryegrass *Lolium multiflorum*	Quick to sprout and grow; lush spring green grass to use alone in pots or as accent plant	Cool weather	2 to 3 inches tall, spreading	Full sun	Medium to high	All zones	None specific	Start from seed in early fall or early spring; excellent winter color
Scarlet Sage *Salvia splendens* Blaze of Fire, Flamenco, Red Hot Sally, Top Burgundy	Branching plant with intense summer flow-ers of red, rose, salmon, purple, and white, along with lush foliage; attracts hummingbirds	Warm weather	8 inches to 1½ feet tall, 3 to 6 inches wide	Full sun (red types); all others, partial shade	Medium to high	All zones	None specific	Plant in spring, after last frost; pinch back new plants to promote branching; cut off old flower spikes

ANNUALS

NAME/ SELECTIONS	FEATURES	SEASON	NATURAL SIZE	LIGHT	WATER	RANGE	PESTS/ DISEASES	COMMENTS
Snapdragon *Antirrhinum majus* Bells Series, Chimes Series, Liberty Series, Rocket Series, Sonnet Series	Old-fashioned favorite; tall flower spikes in ice-cream colors; dependable fall and spring color; dwarf types do not need staking	Cool weather into warm weather; flowers fade in midsummer	6 inches to 3 feet tall, 6 to 8 inches wide	Full sun to partial shade	Medium to high	All zones	Root rot	Set out plants in early fall in Zones 7 to 9, in early spring farther north; cut back faded spikes and others will appear
Sweet Alyssum *Lobularia maritima* Carpet of Snow, Snow Crystals, Tiny Tim	Old-fashioned fragrant mat of blooms in early spring; good companion with petunias and pansies	Cool weather	3 to 8 inches tall, 6 to 12 inches wide	Full sun	Medium to high	All zones	Root rot	Start from plants or seed in early to mid-spring; transplants tolerate light frost; trim off old flowers to prolong bloom
Viola *Viola cornuta* **Johnny-jump-up** *Viola tricolor*	Called minipansies; charming small flowers in white, violet, yellow, lavender, and multicolored; good with spring bulbs	Cool weather	4 to 8 inches tall, 2 to 4 inches wide	Full sun	Medium	All zones	None specific	Start from transplants in fall before first frost; feed with nitrate-based fertilizer to promote flowering
Wax Begonia *Begonia* x *semperflorens-cultorum* BRONZE-LEAFED: Cocktail Series GREEN-LEAFED: Encore, Olympia	Mounding summer color with red, pink, white, salmon, and bicolored flowers; bronze-leafed types will take full sun if watered well	Warm weather	6 to 12 inches tall, equally wide	Full sun to partial shade	Medium	All zones; perennial in Zones 8 to 10	None specific	Set transplants out after last frost; add controlled-release fertilizer in midsummer

PERENNIALS

NAME/SPECIES & SELECTIONS	FEATURES	SEASON	NATURAL SIZE	LIGHT	WATER	RANGE	PESTS/ DISEASES	COMMENTS
Aster *Aster* hybrids MICHAELMAS DAISY (*A. novae-angliae, A. novi-belgii*); *A. DUMOSUS* HYBRIDS: Fanny's, Harrington's Pink, Hella Lacy	Stout-stemmed plant with fall flowers in daisylike shapes of blue, purple, and pink; attracts butterflies	Warm weather; blooms in fall	1 to 3 feet tall, 1 to 2 feet wide	Full sun	Medium	Zones 5 to 8	Mildew	Start from transplants in spring; pair with silvery plants or daylilies
Autumn Fern *Dryopteris erythrosora*	Exotic; one of the few evergreen outdoor ferns; green fronds have overtones of copper, pink, yellow, and then rusty brown	All seasons	2 feet tall, equally wide	Partial to full shade	Medium to high	Zones 6 to 8	None specific	Start from transplants in spring or fall; easy to grow; spreads by rhizomes
Chrysanthemum *Chrysanthemum morifolium* Garden mums	Classic color for fall; mounds of flowers in white, pink, purple, yellow, rust, and burgundy; attracts butterflies	Warm weather; blooms in fall	1 to 2 feet tall, equally wide	Full sun to partial shade	Medium	Zones 5 to 9	Aphids	Start with transplants in early spring or large pots in late summer; pinch back tips to promote sturdy plants

PERENNIALS

NAME/SPECIES & SELECTIONS	FEATURES	SEASON	NATURAL SIZE	LIGHT	WATER	RANGE	PESTS/ DISEASES	COMMENTS
Coreopsis *Coreopsis species* and hybrids Bigflower, Dwarf-eared, Lanceleaf, Threadleaf	Slender green stalks topped with gold or yellow sunflowers; attracts butterflies	Warm weather; different selections bloom in spring, summer, and fall	10 inches to 3 feet tall, 10 inches to 2 feet wide	Full sun to partial shade	Medium	Zones 4 to 9	Root rot	Start from transplants in fall or spring; deadhead to promote flowering; companion for lamb's ears and petunias
Daylily *Hemerocallis* hybrids Numerous available; Black-eyed Stella, Happy Returns, Lemon Daylily (fragrant), Stella de Oro	Showy summer-blooming lilies with clumps of arching, grassy foliage; select reblooming and dwarf types	Warm weather; blooms in summer, but foliage looks fine in spring and fall	8 inches to 2 feet tall, equally wide	Full sun to partial shade	Medium	Zones 3 to 10; some selections are ever-green in Lower South	None specific	Start from transplants in spring or fall; give plenty of room; dead-head flowers daily
Dianthus (Cheddar Pink) *Dianthus gratianopolitanus* Bath's Pink, Little Boy Blue, Little Joe, Rose Bowl, Tiny Rubies	Old-fashioned, blue-gray matting plant with fragrant, carnation-like spring flowers in white, pink to ruby; do not confuse with annual dianthus	All seasons, evergreen; blooms heavily in spring if flowers are deadheaded	3 to 15 inches tall, mat-forming	Full sun	Medium	Zones 4 to 8	Root rot	Start from transplants in fall or early spring; good drainage a must; works as good ground cover under larger plants; place where fragrance can be enjoyed
English Ivy *Hedera helix* Many types with variety of leaf sizes and variegation	Classic evergreen vine with lobed leaves; comes in variegated forms; good for cover-ing topiary forms; use as trailer	All seasons	6 to 12 inches tall, vining	Partial sun to full shade	Medium	Zones 3 to 10	Spider mites	Start from transplants or rooted cuttings in spring, summer, or fall; prune to maintain size; lovely white flowers
Fountain Grass *Pennisetum alopecuroides* Cassian, Hameln, Little Bunny, Moudry, Oriental Fountain Grass (*P. orientale*)	Graceful, grassy clump with coppery pink or purplish flower spikes on 3- to 4-foot stems can last until frost; striking specimen	Warm weather; blooms in summer	1½ to 4 feet tall; equally wide	Full sun	Medium	Zones 7 to 10	None specific	Start from transplants in spring or fall; cut back in late winter to promote spring growth; do not overfertilize; needs good drainage
Hosta *Hosta* hybrids Hundreds of selec-tions available; Antioch, August Moon, Blue Wedg-wood, Royal Standard (fragrant)	Elegant, large-leafed plants prized for showy foliage in blue, green, yellow, and variegated; delicate blooms	Warm weather	2 to 4 feet tall, equally wide	Partial to full shade	Medium to high	Zones 3 to 8	None specific	Start from transplants in spring; use large types as specimens, smaller types as com-panions to other shade- lovers
Lamb's Ears *Stachys byzantina*	Cottage-garden favorite; evergreen; mat-forming plant with silver-gray velvety foliage; tall lavender flower spikes in late spring	All seasons	6 to 15 inches tall, spreading	Full sun	Medium	Zones 4 to 8	Root rot	Start from transplants in fall or spring; keep plants trimmed back; divide every 2 to 3 years; cut off flower spikes after blooming

PERENNIALS

NAME/SPECIES & SELECTIONS	FEATURES	SEASON	NATURAL SIZE	LIGHT	WATER	RANGE	PESTS/ DISEASES	COMMENTS
Liriope, Big Blue *Liriope muscari* Many selections available; Evergreen Giant, Majestic, Monroe White, Silvery Sunproof	Simple ground cover becomes striking in a container; evergreen, with variegated forms; lavender or white flower spikes	All seasons; blooms in summer	8 inches to 2 feet tall, equally wide	Full sun to full shade, depending on selection	Medium	Zones 5 to 10	None specific	Start from transplants in fall, spring, or summer; use alone or as evergreen feature in mixed planting; low maintenance
Periwinkle *Vinca* Common periwinkle (*V. minor*), Greater periwinkle (*V. major*)	Lustrous, leafy evergreen vine with lavender blue or white flowers; variegated forms available; Greater periwinkle has large, showy leaves	All seasons; blooms in spring	4 to 8 inches tall, vining	Partial to full shade	Medium	Zones 4 to 8; Greater periwinkle is better adapted to Lower South	None specific	Start from transplants in fall or spring; keep pruned to maintain size and shape; good trailing accent plant
Ribbon Grass *Phalaris arundinacea* Dwarf Garters, Mervyn Feesey, Picta (white striped)	Tough, old-fashioned bamboolike grass; deep green ages to pale buff in fall; comes in variegated forms	Warm weather	2 to 3 feet tall, 6 inches wide, clump forming	Partial to full shade	High	Zones 6 to 10	None specific	Set out as transplants in early spring or late summer for fall; keep well watered; prune back weak canes
Rose Verbena *Verbena canadensis* Homestead Purple	Low-growing, branching native with minty-looking leaves; clusters of rosy or purple flowers; attracts butterflies; white, pink, and purple selections available	Warm weather	6 inches to 2 feet tall, 2 feet wide	Full sun	Low to medium	Zones 6 to 10; move to sheltered area in winter in Zones 6 and 7	Mildew, spider mites	Start with transplants in spring; provide air circulation; good for hanging baskets; often grown as an annual
Showy Sedum *Sedum spectabile* Autumn Joy, Brilliant, Meteor, Star Dust	Old-fashioned succulent; gray-green leaves with late summer blooms, turning pink, bronze, and then rust; attracts butterflies	Warm weather; blooms in fall	1 to 2 feet tall, 1 to 2 feet wide	Full sun	Medium	Zones 4 to 10	Root rot	Start with transplants in spring; pinch back leggy plants; good "filler" in border, or use as accent to mark entry to deck or patio
Sweet Flag *Acorus gramineus* Ogon, Pusillus, Variegatus	Exotic, featuring fans of grasslike leaves; comes in yellow, green, or variegated; good vertical accent	Warm weather	2 inches to 1½ feet tall, equally wide	Full sun to partial shade	High	Zones 6 to 8	None specific	Start from transplants in spring; use alone or in mixed plantings; do not allow to dry out

Hosta and white impatiens

Bulbs

These potted rain lilies soften the hard lines of brick steps.

Most bulbs produce small to medium-sized plants that are well suited to containers. Valued as seasonal accents in the garden, bulbs grow foliage for a limited number of months, bloom for only a few weeks, and then disappear from sight for the rest of the year.

When they are at their peak, display them in pots, window boxes, or hanging baskets and put them out of sight when blossoms fade. For year-round interest, tuck them into pots or planters large enough to accommodate annuals and perennials or even trees or shrubs. Place the planter by the door to welcome guests and to serve as a marker of the changing seasons. Or set out a series of small containers planted just with bulbs. For example, you can plant a container for each season, filling it with spring blooming crocus and daffodils, summer-blooming rain lilies and spider lilies, autumn crocus, and winter paperwhites.

Old-fashioned favorites, bulbs create seasonal splashes in the garden.

This pot of paperwhites anchored with Spanish moss provides winter fragrance.

These caladium tubers are ready to plant in middle to late spring.

Growing Bulbs in Containers

Containers make good homes for bulbs for a number of reasons. They allow you to provide the perfect drainage that some bulbs, such as lilies, demand. They also help you adapt bulbs to climates where temperatures limit their success. For example, in mild climates where winter is short, tulips grow better in pots because the bulbs are exposed to more winter cold than they would be in the ground. In cooler climates, pots allow you to grow tropical bulbs from year to year; these cold-tender plants would freeze in the ground, but pots allow you the flexibility to move the plants indoors in the winter.

Because of this climate control, all you need to successfully grow bulbs is to start with healthy bulbs and appropriate containers.

Types of Bulbs

A specialized group of perennial plants, bulbs include a number of plants that are not true bulbs—plants that have **corms, rhizomes, tubers,** and **tuberous roots** as their storage organs. These are thickened parts of the plant that store the nutrients necessary to complete the plant's life cycles. The important thing is not to be confused by their names; for the practical purposes of gardening, you can handle them like a true bulb, such as a tulip or a daffodil.

While the chart that begins on page 77 designates plants started from a corm, rhizome, tuber, or tuberous root (just to be botanically correct), remember that in general you can think of them all as bulbs.

Buying Bulbs

If you purchase your bulbs at a garden center, be sure to get them as soon as they are available, even if you must wait to plant them. Bulbs are very seasonal and frequently are offered for sale only a few weeks of the year. However, catalogues offer them early for shipment at planting time. Dutch bulbs, such as daffodils, hyacinths, and tulips, usually arrive in September, but in most of the South you should wait until October or November to plant them. Summer bulbs arrive early in the spring; plant them as soon as the ground can be worked.

Choose a bulb as you would choose an onion in the supermarket. The bulb should be firm and without mold or rot on the outside; a bulb that feels soft or spongy when squeezed may be diseased or old and dehydrated. Store bulbs in a cool, dry place until you are ready to plant.

Choosing Containers for Bulbs

When selecting a container in which to grow bulbs, remember that plants in pots are more subject to extremes of temperature than are those in the ground. To minimize the stress from heat and drought in the summer, use large containers (at least 16 inches in diameter) that hold ample amounts of soil. However, some tropical bulbs may benefit from the warmer temperatures in the summer. Likewise, spring bulbs, such as tulips grown at the southern limits of their range, perform better with a few degrees of winter chilling.

No matter which container you choose, be sure it permits good drainage. Bulbs will rot quickly if left sitting in soggy soil for any period of time.

Planting Bulbs in Containers

Once you've decided where to place your containers, select bulbs that will thrive in the conditions of your site. Pay close attention to how much sunlight the spot gets. Plants at the limit of their range may benefit from the extra shade and slightly cooler temperatures found close to the foundation on the eastern or northern side of the house. Some summer bulbs, such as hyacinths, narcissus, and tulips, prefer the additional heat and the strong sunlight of a southern or western exposure.

Potentially, all bulbs are perennials, and with proper care, most will return and bloom for many years. This holds true for containerized bulbs as well, provided you simulate ground conditions. Some, however, should be discarded as their primary show is for only one season. Consult the chart on pages 77 and 78 for specific planting information on the bulbs you wish to plant. This chart will help you determine the ideal width and depth of a container for single bulbs or figure out how many bulbs you can plant in a pot of a given size. For a bulb to perform as a perennial, it must be planted at a specific depth in the soil and at an adequate distance from other bulbs in the container. This allows the bulb to receive the proper amount of heat or cold to stimulate flowering and have enough space to grow roots to support next year's flowers and foliage.

Selecting a Potting Soil

For potting bulbs, use a quality growing mix that drains well. To reduce the need for watering in the summer, add a water-retaining polymer, following manufacturer's directions. Always lightly

Caladiums and asparagus fern in a white pot add color and texture to a shady area.

Potted crocus and hyacinths provide color in late winter and early spring.

moisten the mix before placing it in the container. Stir in a small amount of water; continue adding water and stirring until the mix is moist enough to clump when squeezed. To prevent the potting mix from flushing out the drainage hole when you water, cover the hole with a layer of coarse gravel or pot rubble or with a piece of coarse screening. If none of these are available, you can use a coffee filter or a layer of straw.

There is enough room in large planters or half-barrels to plant several layers of bulbs, especially if the plants have different spacing requirements and their periods of active growth occur during different seasons. Add other plants for color when the bulbs are dormant. (See Overfilling a Container at right.) Perennial bulbs, such as lily-of-the-Nile, need more room to grow because the bulbs fatten for next year's bloom. When potting perennial bulbs, make sure the container holds enough mix to accommodate the plants' roots; then place the bulbs on top, allowing standard spacing around them. Cover the bulbs to the proper depth with additional potting soil, firming it with your fingers. Water with a gentle mist to settle the potting mix around the bulbs.

Give long-blooming lily-of-the-Nile, a bulb-like perennial, enough room for its roots to grow, and you can leave it in a container for years without repotting.

When you treat bulbs, such as tulips, as annuals, plant them closer together to create showy displays.

Treating Bulbs As Annuals

You may treat certain bulbs as annuals because of the difficulty of keeping them for more than a season. These include bulbs that aren't well suited to your climate—tulips in the Lower and Gulf South fall into this category, as might tropical bulbs that aren't reliably frost hardy, such as caladiums. You can plant these bulbs treated as annuals right next to each other in a pot or layer upon layer within a container to ensure a spectacular display of densely packed blossoms. Once the blooms fade, discard the plants since they cannot be counted on to bloom the following year.

Plant spring-blooming bulbs, such as daffodils, in containers as late as January or early February. The bulbs will usually be exposed to enough cold at this time to meet their chilling requirements to break dormancy, as temperatures are more frigid in pots than in the ground.

Buying late in the season will limit your choices, of course, but bulbs are usually priced for clearance at that time and are good values as annuals, but only if they are still firm and in good condition.

Overfilling a Container

When treating bulbs as annuals for a onetime display, you can disregard the recommendations having to do with depth and spacing. Instead, feel free to pack as many bulbs as you can fit into the container.

1. Creating a mixed planting of bulbs is like assembling a layer cake. Place gravel and a little bonemeal at the base of the pot for the bottom layer (top right). Then add a couple of inches of soil in which to grow the first layer of bulbs. Sprinkle with bulb booster or bonemeal.

2. Since daffodil and tulip bulbs are the largest bulbs, they need to be planted deepest in the container (center right). Notice that they are set close together because they are being grown as annuals and will be discarded once they have bloomed. Then add another inch or two of soil and sprinkle with bonemeal or bulb booster.

3. Place more tulip bulbs and a layer of hyacinth bulbs, followed by soil (bottom right). Continue adding bulbs, planting smaller, earlier flowering ones, such as crocus, last of all.

After the bulbs bloom, transplant them to appropriate spots in the garden. They should rebloom when transplanted at the proper spacing. Replant the pots with summer annuals when the bulbs are finished blooming.

Care and Maintenance

Keep bulbs moist until foliage appears; then water regularly during the growing season and the blooming periods. Rainfall may provide enough moisture for winter- and spring-blooming bulbs, but check the soil regularly for dryness. When they aren't dormant, bulbs need to be watered once or twice a week. Get in the habit of sticking your index finger into the pot whenever you pass by; apply water when the potting mix is dry to the depth of 1 to 2 inches.

Fertilize spring bulbs in the fall, just before their foliage appears, by scratching a controlled-release bulb food, such as 9-9-6, into the surface of the potting mix. Spring-blooming bulbs, such as daffodils, benefit from another application immediately after they begin to flower.

To ensure blooms in the coming year, let foliage yellow and fade naturally when the bulbs finish flowering. You can move these unsightly pots to an out-of-the-way spot or tuck them among the shrubbery.

In the winter, leave hardy bulbs outdoors in their pots. Place these containers in a sheltered location, burying them under straw or mulch when cold weather threatens. Be sure to remove the mulch or the straw as soon as the weather warms, or rot may result. Move the pots of the most tender bulbs or tropical bulbs to a basement, a garage, a laundry room, or another frostproof location for the winter. Do not feed these bulbs and water them only sparingly.

These daffodils and hyacinths pushed up through the top layer of soil planted with pansies to create a spring show. Keep them well watered.

BULBS

NAME/SPECIES & SELECTIONS	FEATURES	SEASON	NATURAL SIZE	LIGHT	WATER	RANGE	PLANTING TIPS AND COMMENTS
Amaryllis *Hippeastrum* hybrids Butterfly amaryllis (*H. papilio*), Mexican lily (*H. reginae*), St. Joseph's lily (*H. x johnsonii*) Dutch hybrids	Old-fashioned lily with 2 to 8 flowers on strong stems, 8 to 9 inches in diameter; blooms in red, orange, pink, salmon, and white; St. Joseph's lily is fragrant	Spring	1 to 2 feet tall, equally wide	Full sun to light shade	Medium, high in full sun; when flowers fade, cut off stems, keep watering to encourage leaf growth; when leaves yellow, stop watering to allow plants to dry out	Zones 8 to 10; annual in other zones	Set bulb in potting soil, allowing 2 inches between bulb and edge of pot; set upper half of bulb above soil surface. Firm soil with fingertips. For pots outdoors, plant deeper, covering bulbs with soil. Set out November through February in rich, sandy mix enriched with bulb booster. Overwinter indoors north of Zone 8.
Achimenes *Achimenes species* Fairy Pink, Purple King, Rosy Red	Tender perennial; trailing habit with tubular flowers in blue, pink, or shades of purple, 1 to 3 inches in diameter; good for window box or hanging basket	Summer	6 inches to 2 feet tall, equally wide	Shade	Medium	Zones 7 to 11	When plants are 3 inches high, set them ½ to 1 inch deep, 4 inches apart. Set out rhizomes in March or April; protect from sun and wind. In fall, dig rhizomes, let dry, and store in cool, dry place; repot in spring. Purple King hardy in outdoor pots 10°F to 0°F.
Caladium *Caladium species* SHADE-LOVING: Candidum, Fanny Munson, Frieda Hemple, Pink Beauty, Pink Symphony SUN-TOLERANT: Aaron, Fire Chief, Lance Whorton, Pink Cloud, Red Flash, Red Frill, Rose Bud, White Queen	Popular, tropical foliage plant; exotic heart-shaped leaves, banded or blotched in red, white, silver, bronze, and green	Summer to fall	2 to 4 feet tall, equally wide	Full sun to shade	Medium	Zone 10; annual in other zones	For 1 or 2 large tubers, use 7-inch pot filled three-quarters full with potting soil. Place tuber on top and cover with 2 inches of soil. Start tubers indoors in March, outdoors in May. Add 1 teaspoon fish meal at planting. To overwinter, bring pots indoors before first frost in fall.
Crocus *Crocus species* Dutch crocus (*C. vernus*), Saffron crocus (*C. sativus*)	Small, cup-shaped flowers in wide range of colors: white, yellows, blues, purples, and pinks; dainty, vigorous bloomers	Late winter to early spring; saffron crocus blooms in fall	4 to 6 inches tall, equally wide	Full sun to partial shade	Medium	Zones 3 to 8	Set corms 2 to 3 inches deep, at least 3 inches apart; if planting as annuals, set corms 1 inch apart. Plant in fall; for impact, group 5 or more in shallow dishes or window boxes.
Daffodil *Narcissus species* LARGE-FLOWERED: Carlton, February Gold, Geranium, Hawera, Ice Follies SMALL-FLOWERED: Tête à Tête, Thalia	Great variety of form and size in these bulbous flowers: white, yellow, and bicolored, including orange centers; some fragrant, especially paperwhites; plant different types for 3 months of blooms	Late winter to spring	4 to 20 inches tall, 6 to 8 inches wide	Sun; late-blooming selections last longer in light shade	Medium	Zones 4 to 9	To reuse bulbs, set 5 to 6 inches deep in potting soil; if planting as annuals, set 1 to 2 inches deep, 1 to 2 inches apart. Plant October through December. Flowers will turn to face sun. Let foliage mature and yellow naturally.

BULBS

NAME/SPECIES & SELECTIONS	FEATURES	SEASON	NATURAL SIZE	LIGHT	WATER	RANGE	PLANTING TIPS AND COMMENTS
Gladiolus *Gladiolus species* G. byzantinum, G. primulinus	Striking as central feature of pot with low annuals at base; wide color range; bloom spikes bear ruffled, flared, or double flowers	Spring to fall, depending on planting time	1½ to 5 feet tall, 1 foot wide	Full sun	Medium	Zones 5 to 9	Grow as annuals. Set corms 4 inches deep, 1 to 2 inches apart. Use large, deep container to balance height. Plant in spring. For successive blooms, plant corms at 1- to 2-week intervals for 6 weeks; good vertical accent.
Hyacinth *Hyacinthus orientalis* Delft Blue, Mont Blanc, Pink Pearl	Highly fragrant, tightly clustered spikes of flowers in white, blue, purple, red, pink, yellow, or salmon	Spring	6 to 12 inches tall, 6 inches wide	Full sun to partial shade	Medium	Zones 6 to 9	Set bulbs 4 to 6 inches deep, 6 inches apart; if using as annuals, plant 1 to 2 inches deep, 1 to 2 inches apart. Plant October through December. Buy prechilled bulbs or refrigerate 10 to 12 weeks before planting.
Lily-of-the-Nile *Agapanthus species* A. africanus, A. Headbourne hybrids, A. orientalis	Fountainlike clumps of strap-shaped leaves remain attractive after flowering; funnel-shaped flowers in blue or white	Summer	1 to 5 feet tall, 1 to 2 feet wide, depending on species	Full sun to partial shade	High	Zones 7 to 10, depending on species	Set rhizomes 1 inch deep, allowing 2 inches between rhizome and edge of pot. Blooms best when slightly potbound. Best to start with container-grown transplants not bare-root plants. Set out in spring; protect from frost. Overwinter evergreen selections indoors north of Zone 8.
Rain Lily *Zephyranthes species* SPRING-BLOOMING: Z. atamasco; SUMMER-BLOOMING: Z. grandiflora; LATE SUMMER- TO FALL-BLOOMING: Z. candida, Z. citrina	Small, pretty lily, with foliage-like monkey grass; blooms appear after rain or when watered; white, pink, or yellow flowers	Spring to fall, depending on species	8 to 12 inches tall, 8 inches wide	Full sun to light shade	Medium, during growth and bloom	Zone 7 to 10	Set bulbs 1 to 2 inches deep; set close together, such as 12 bulbs per 6- to 7-inch pot. Do not disturb plantings. Plant in early summer or fall, depending on species. Container plants bloom better when slightly potbound.
Spider Lily *Lycoris species* Hurricane lily (L. africana), Magic lily (L. squamigera), Spider lily (L. radiata)	Spidery or trumpet-shaped blooms appear before foliage atop slender, straight stems; plant multiple species for successive bloom; colors include white, yellow, gold, red, and pink	Late summer to fall	1 to 2 feet tall, equally as wide	Full sun to light shade	Medium	Zones 5 to 10, depending on species	Plant 1 to 3 bulbs per pot, depending on size of plant; set 3 to 4 inches deep. Use larger, deep container to balance bulb's height. Plant in late summer to fall. Magic lily (fragrant) is hardiest; use others from Zone 7 south. Blooms better when slightly potbound.
Tulip *Tulipa species* Double Early, Parrot, Rembrandt, Single Early	White, rose, red, orange, yellow, cream, pink, mauve, lilac, purple, maroon and near black colors	March to May, depending on type	6 inches to 2½ feet tall, 8 to 10 inches wide	Full sun; afternoon shade helps late-flowering types last longer	Medium	Zones 3 to 7	Grow as annuals. Put 3 to 5 bulbs in 8-inch pot, 1 to 2 inches deep. Plant November through December. In Zones 8 to 10, buy prechilled bulbs or store in refrigerator 10 to 12 weeks before planting.

Herbs and Vegetables

Few plants reward gardeners as much as herbs and vegetables.

Group plants by their growing requirements. In this creative mixture, edible nasturtiums, herbs, and lettuce share containers.

Once you've sprinkled just-picked basil on homegrown tomatoes or fresh chives on potatoes that you've grown yourself, you'll want even more herbs and vegetables at your fingertips. There's a thrill to serving family or guests vegetables raised in a patio planter. Vegetables and herbs are readily at hand if grown in containers placed in sunny spots near the kitchen. A few cherry tomatoes to wake up a salad, enough peppers to make a jar of vinegar sauce, some rosemary to flavor grilled chicken—these are a few of the delectable results of container gardening.

You can plant ornamental herbs, especially perennial evergreens such as lavender, in containers to display as accents anywhere in the garden.

Lemon-scented herbs, such as lemon balm, lemon grass, lemon thyme, and lemon verbena, make a fragrant summer bouquet.

Growing Herbs in Containers

You can often grow herbs more successfully in containers than in the garden. With a planter, you can better control growing conditions and meet an herb's specific needs. What's more, many herbs are perennial and long-lived, making them suitable to grow as a collection.

There's no need to limit yourself to culinary herbs. Try growing ornamental herbs, which add bright colors and exotic fragrances to a container garden. Ornamental herbs include artemisia, bee balm, feverfew, lavender, and scented geranium (the last two are also used in cooking). Many culinary herbs can be treated as ornamentals.

Plant parsley and basil with flowering annuals for seasonal foliage or grow bay, lavender, or rosemary in separate pots as evergreen plantings. Don't forget to mix in some edible flowers, such as daylily, dianthus, marigold, pansy, and rose, with your containerized herbs. Or put these flowers in separate planters and display them along with potted herbs.

Most herbs need at least a half day of full sunlight; these herbs include lavender, rosemary, sage, and thyme. Just a few herbs, such as cilantro, dill, mint, and parsley, prefer partial or afternoon shade, especially in the summer.

The amount of watering needed depends on the plant and the container. This scented geranium is drought tolerant and thrives in an old clay urn.

After you decide which herbs will do best in the light conditions of your site, determine whether the herbs are warm-weather, cool-weather, or perennial herbs. When planting several herbs in one container, combine those with similar needs and harvest seasons.

Warm-weather: Plant in the spring, after the threat of frost has passed. Warm-weather herbs include basil, marjoram, and summer savory.

Cool-weather: Plant in early spring or late summer, to take advantage of the 6 to 12 weeks of upcoming cool weather of spring and fall. Such herbs include cilantro, dill, and parsley. Some leafy greens, such as parsley, will survive the heat of summer and can be harvested in spring and fall.

Perennial: Plant early in the spring or fall. These herbs include artemisia,* bee balm, burnet,* catnip, chives,* fennel, feverfew, germander,* lavender,* lemon balm, mint,* oregano,* rosemary,* sage,* savory,* tarragon,* and thyme.*

Tender perennials: These herbs are perennial in containers only in Zones 8 and 9. They include bay,* lemon grass, lemon verbena, Mexican mint marigold, rosemary,* and scented geranium. Bay will survive the winter if moved indoors before the first frost. Plant in spring.

* Often evergreen in the South

VEGETABLES BY THE SEASON

Warm-weather: Plant in the spring, after the threat of frost has passed. These vegetables include beans, cucumbers, eggplants, peppers, summer squash, sweet potatoes, and tomatoes.

Cool-weather: Plant in early spring or late summer, to take advantage of the 6 to 12 weeks of cool weather that precede the extreme heat or cold of the following season. Examples include beets, broccoli, collards, gourmet salad greens, kale, lettuce, bunching onions, peas, potatoes, radicchio, spinach, and Swiss chard. Such leafy greens as Swiss chard prefer the cool temperatures of spring and fall and, therefore, have two harvest seasons.

These young lettuce plants are thinned through harvesting.

Growing Vegetables in Containers

The goal of growing vegetables in containers is not necessarily to raise large quantities but to grow fresh vegetables that taste better than those sold at the grocery store.

Most vegetables require full sunlight, so look around for the sunniest available spot to put your containers. Warm-weather crops, such as peppers and tomatoes, require six to eight hours of sunlight per day to do well. Leafy crops, such as collards, gourmet salad greens, and lettuce, survive with four to six hours of sunlight but do not grow as vigorously. An area shaded by deciduous trees in the summer may receive enough light in the fall, the winter, and early spring for these cool-season crops, since patterns of sunlight shift as leaf density changes. Plants in containers can be moved from place to place to maximize sun exposure. Place heavy pots on casters to facilitate moving.

After deciding on a site, choose the right vegetable or mix of vegetables for container plantings. Many of the most popular vegetables—beans, gourmet salad greens, peas, peppers, squash, and tomatoes—thrive in containers. To improve your chances of success, grow early-maturing, compact, dwarf, or baby types of your favorite vegetables. (See the chart on pages 93–96 for suggestions.) However, do not hesitate to experiment with larger selections; just remember that you will have to stake some of them and water them more often.

Since containerized plants need a steady supply of moisture to produce well, place the plants where you will see them several times a day. This proximity helps you remember to water and allows you to spot wilting and insect problems before they get out of hand. Ideal locations are outside the kitchen window and along the pathways you travel when entering and leaving the house.

You don't have to sacrifice aesthetics to include vegetables in your container garden. Foliage and vegetables can be as attractive as flowers, especially when they are displayed in handsome containers. Edible flowers, such as daylilies, nasturtiums, and pansies, add color to plantings. Here are some other suggestions:

• Plant eggplants, peppers, or tomatoes in separate pots, placing the containers on a sunny deck or patio. Stake each plant with a wooden stick, a piece of bamboo, or other support.

• For a focal point in the landscape, plant Swiss chard, ornamental kale, radicchio, red lettuce, or other vegetables with boldly colored leaves in a single large container.

• Add an accent of trailing green-and-purple foliage to a planter of annuals by tucking in a sweet potato plant.

• Secure a decorative trellis or a topiary form in a sturdy pot; then plant purple pole beans, scarlet runner beans, or snow peas at the base of the structure. You will have the pleasure of beautiful blossoms, colorful butterflies, and a delicious vegetable.

Three sticks of bamboo, tied at the top to form a tepee, provide a handy trellis for baby cucumber plants.

A cool-weather annual, lettuce is one of the stars of a container garden because it is as pretty as it is tasty.

An old dough bowl holds a planting of oregano, rosemary, sage, and thyme. These herbs require excellent drainage and tolerate drought, making them prime candidates for large, shallow containers.

Choosing Containers

Because the roots of herbs generally do not grow very deep, they fare well in shallow containers. Most herbs need excellent drainage and, therefore, grow best in porous clay pots that do not retain water for a long time. A few herbs, such as basil, burnet, cilantro, dill, lemon balm, mint, and parsley, have high moisture requirements and should be grown in less porous foam or plastic pots. Woody herbs—such as bay or rosemary—that spend several seasons in the same pot need containers that hold at least 5 gallons of soil in order for the plants to develop a large root system.

Successfully growing vegetables in containers requires careful consideration of the pot size and the soil volume. Containers should be large enough to avoid undue stress during periods of extreme temperatures. (See pages 24–33 for more information on choosing the right container.) For most vegetables, select containers that will hold at least 5 gallons of soil—pots that are at least 16 inches in diameter and equally deep. Leafy crops, such as lettuce, spinach, and Swiss chard generally grow well in wide, shallow, boatlike containers; however, these types of containers may dry out too quickly when the weather heats up. Root crops, such as beets and carrots, must have deep pots—at least 1 foot deeper than their mature roots. Pole beans, squash, tomatoes, and other vegetables with sprawling root systems require pots that are at least 20 inches in diameter.

Containers come in a variety of materials, clay being the most popular; however, plastic and resin pots are good choices for growing vegetables, since they slow the evaporation of moisture from the potting soil. These containers are also lightweight, an advantage if you plan to move the pots. Wooden or concrete containers are other options, but you have to water plants in them more often, at least in the summer. All pots must have drainage holes because vegetables will not survive long in waterlogged soil. Garden-supply stores and catalogues now offer self-watering and self-feeding containers for patio gardens.

Planting Herbs and Vegetables in Pots

The season of the year for planting herbs and vegetables varies, depending on the type of plant, the time required before it is ready for harvesting, and its cold or heat tolerance. In general, plant cool-weather types in late summer for a fall crop and again in late winter or early spring for a spring crop. Plant warm-weather types in late spring, after the threat of frost has passed. (See the boxes on pages 81 and 82 for a list of cool-weather and warm-weather herbs and vegetables.)

Perennial herbs and some vegetables are slow to grow from seed. Start with transplants whenever possible, as they grow to full size more quickly than do plants grown from seed. (See the box on page 86 for some exceptions.) For heirloom selections or plants not found locally, be prepared to start plants directly from seed.

Since pots are heavy after being filled with soil and plant material, set your container at your selected site before planting. To prepare the pot, cover the drainage hole with pieces of coarse screen so that the soil and the roots remain inside the container. Mix controlled-release fertilizer into the potting soil if the soil doesn't already contain it. Add moistened potting mix, filling the pot to within 2 inches of the rim.

To get a transplant started, carefully remove it from the container. (Do not pull the plant out by its stem.) If roots are heavily matted, make a cut in the bottom of the root ball and gently tease the tangled roots apart. Place the plant in the new pot so that the surface of the root ball is within 2 inches of the rim. Fill in around the root ball with potting mix, firming the surface with your fingers. Level off the mix to within 2 inches of the rim of the pot. Do not fill the pot too full, or soil will wash out when you water. Also, do not set the plant too high (a common mistake).

After planting, water the transplant thoroughly three times; then feed it with a water-soluble fertilizer, such as 20-20-20, to promote new root and foliage growth. Apply a ½-inch layer of mulch to keep roots moist and cool in the summer and to add an attractive touch to the planting. Make sure the mulch is several inches away from the crown of the plant to avoid rot.

If planting different vegetables or herbs together, remember to match plants with similar growing conditions and seasons. For example, plant cool-weather annual herbs, such as cilantro, dill, or parsley, with cool-weather vegetables, such as beets, carrots, or radishes. When grouping several plants in a container, be sure to maintain the proper spacing, or plants will be stunted. Set tall plants at the back of a container to keep them from overshadowing shorter ones. Also, stagger your plantings so that you can harvest vegetables at different times in the growing season. For example, plant tomatoes in the spring, in early summer, and again in midsummer.

A bay tree may start out small and grow slowly, but eventually it will need to be moved to a large pot. In a container, this evergreen herb makes a handsome addition to a border.

Herbs: Almost all herbs are available as transplants. If you wish to start some from seed, try basil, cilantro, dill, or parsley.

Large-seeded vegetables: Grow beans, cucumbers, edible-podded peas, and squash from seed, sowing at the proper spacing. No thinning is necessary.

Small-seeded vegetables: Sow carrots, lettuce, radishes, and spinach from seed, taking care to thin seedlings once they are 1 to 2 inches tall.

Sow seeds as if they were in the ground, following recommendations on the packet. Keep the surface of the soil evenly moist during germination. Stretch plastic wrap over the top of the container to maintain the moisture level needed for seed starting. Once seedlings are 1 to 2 inches tall, thin them to about half the suggested spacing. When thinning, pinch seedlings off at the soil line.

Care and Maintenance

Vegetables grow rapidly, therefore, they require more maintenance than other plants if they are to produce well. The most important task when raising vegetables in pots is watering. If you skip a watering or two, your plants will wilt and may not produce properly. Herbs, on the other hand, require less maintenance and are more drought tolerant than vegetables. Here are a few guidelines to follow for growing herbs and vegetables in containers successfully.

Herbs

Planting herbs in containers is easier than planting in the ground. However, containers are less forgiving if you forget to water or fertilize, so place pots in a location where you will notice them.

Watering. In late fall until midspring, when it is cool and often rainy, water herbs about once a week. From late spring to early fall, when it is hot and sometimes dry, water herbs two to three times a week or whenever the potting mix is dry to the touch.

Do not let the soil dry out and the plant wilt, because most herbs will have difficulty recovering. Check herbs daily that are in direct sunlight. Water in the morning so that the foliage dries out before the temperature rises. Take care with such herbs as lavender, rosemary, sage, tarragon, and thyme, which are susceptible to fungal diseases, including root rot, in the South. Let these herbs dry out between waterings. Also, make certain these plants have plenty of air circulation. Consider mulching around the crown with a ring of coarse sand or small pebbles to ensure that water doesn't remain on the soil surface long. To avoid getting the foliage wet, water only at the base of the plants.

Use a watering wand or a nozzle with a fine spray to help keep soil from splashing out of the pot.

Fertilizing. In general, herbs need only a little fertilizer. Add an all-purpose controlled-release fertilizer to the soil at planting and again midway through the growing season. (Do not use leftover controlled-release lawn food as it contains too much nitrogen.) To stimulate new growth, apply liquid fertilizer after cutting a plant back severely for harvest.

Harvesting. Pinch back leaves regularly on herbs to promote new branching and growth. Harvest herbs on a sunny morning when the oils have their strongest flavor. For woody herbs, such as lavender, lemon verbena, or rosemary, harvest as though you were pruning a small shrub; eliminate dead wood, remove no more than a third of the plan, and take care to preserve the plant's natural shape.

With such annual herbs as basil and dill, cut the plant back by one-third several times during the growing season or harvest the complete plant before it goes to seed in early summer or before it is threatened by frost. Woody perennial herbs, such as rosemary or thyme, should not be harvested heavily during periods of extreme heat or during the winter. However, light harvesting year-round of leafy evergreens, such as oregano and sage, is recommended.

Pinching the blooms from basil will keep the plant growing new leaves and stems until frost.

Just a few containers can yield a generous harvest of herb sprigs such as marjoram (left) and oregano (right).

87

Potted tomatoes, such as these gourmet pear (named for their shape) tomatoes, need a consistent supply of water.

Vegetables

Just as regular care of a garden keeps it growing and producing, regular care of container vegetables keeps them healthy and growing.

Watering. Unlike vegetables in the ground, vegetables in pots are not able to spread out their roots in search of water. During cool, cloudy periods in the fall to the spring, you may need to water only once or twice a week. In the hot weather of summer, however, water vegetables every day. Because a uniform supply of moisture is so important, you may want to attach a drip system on a timer to an outdoor spigot. Do not allow the soil to dry out between waterings.

Fertilizing. Constant watering leaches fertilizer from the soil. Plants such as tomatoes, which produce an abundance of fruit, need a regular application of water-soluble fertilizer (20-20-20), in addition to the controlled-release fertilizer mixed into the soil at planting. Generally, feed plants every 7 to 10 days after the first fruits appear until they are harvested. Follow the directions on the fertilizer package for the type of plant you are growing.

Additional care. Many vegetables are sensitive to sudden drops in temperature. Cover them with a cloche (such as a nursery pot, a cardboard box, or a milk jug with the bottom cut out) to keep them warm in the spring and to protect them from early frosts in the fall; be sure to remove the cloche the following day or the plants may be killed by the heat. Other options include moving the pots to a sheltered location if the temperature drops or insulating the pots by surrounding them with bales of pine straw.

In addition, vegetables are susceptible to a variety of diseases and insect problems. Minimize soilborne diseases by using a quality potting mix. Also, select resistant selections whenever possible and watch for evidence of insects throughout the spring, the summer, and the fall, when pests are most prevalent. Handpick such caterpillars as tomato hornworms or parsleyworms. Spray sucking insects, such as aphids and whiteflies, with a mild soap insecticide. (See pages 124 and 125 for more information on pests and diseases.) Do not spray vegetables with anything that is not listed as approved for use on vegetables on the product label. If in doubt, call your county Extension Service agent.

Harvesting. Cultivate vegetables regularly; if you stop harvesting, fruit will become oversize and tough, and plants will cease producing. For baby vegetables, simply harvest when crops are small. Remove diseased portions that could infect the rest of the plant or sap its energy. And feed plants regularly during the harvest season. Pick vegetables in early morning, when they have the highest water content and are at their freshest. At the end of the growing season (whether warm weather or cool weather), harvest the entire crop.

Small tomatoes are among the best types of vegetables to grow in containers.

Container gardening is a great way to introduce children to the cycles of nature and to teach them how food is grown. Spring or summer vacation is an ideal time to create a container garden. The gardening and harvesting process can even be documented for a school science project.

Select easy-to-grow, quick-producing vegetables so that the children's efforts will be rewarded in a short time. In the spring, try raising quick-growing radishes from seed. Thin the plants so that they produce sizable roots. In the summer, try planting a pizza garden—include basil, cherry tomatoes, garlic chives, and oregano—starting with transplants. Invite the children to keep a garden diary in which they describe plant care and growth. Take photos of the young farmers picking their first crop.

HERBS

NAME/SPECIES & SELECTIONS	FEATURES	SEASON	NATURAL SIZE	LIGHT	WATER	RANGE	PESTS/DISEASES	COMMENTS
Artemisia *Artemisia species* Powis Castle	Ornamental, evergreen perennial; gray-green or silver foliage; aromatic, dried leaves used in sachets	All seasons	1 to 5 feet tall, 1 to 2 feet wide	Full sun	Medium	Zones 4 to 8	Fungus	Start from transplants in spring or fall; use as evergreen foliage plant; pair with bright colors
Basil *Ocimum basilicum* Lemon basil, Purple basil, Sweet basil	Bushy, aromatic annual, grown for savory foliage; used in pesto; comes in green or purple and in many scents and flavors	Warm weather	6 inches to 3 feet tall, 6 to 12 inches wide	Full sun to light shade	High	All zones	Fungus, Japanese beetle	Start from transplants in spring, 2 to 4 weeks after last frost; keep flowers pinched back; harvest as needed, but harvest entire plant before frost
Bay *Laurus nobilis*	Semitropical evergreen shrublike tree; glossy leaves prized for flavoring soups; winter hardy in pots in Zones 8 to 10	All seasons	12 to 40 feet tall, 8 to 10 feet wide	Full sun to partial shade; likes afternoon shade in summer	Low to medium	All zones; overwinter indoors in Zone 7 and north	Scale	Start from small plants in spring; shelter from cold winds and hot afternoon sun
Bee Balm *Monarda didyma* Adam, Mahogany, Marshall's Delight, Violet Queen	Ornamental, flowering native perennial with showy (edible) flowers in red, pink, and lavender; attracts bees, butterflies, and hummingbirds	Warm weather	2 to 3 feet tall, 6 to 12 inches wide	Full sun to partial shade	Medium	Zones 4 to 9	Powdery mildew	Start from transplants in spring or fall; great for summer color and for attracting wildlife
Burnet *Poterium sanguisorba*	Pretty, delicate perennial with delightful cucumber-flavored leaves for salads; evergreen in the Lower South	Cool weather	1 to 3 feet tall, 1 foot wide	Full sun to partial shade; likes afternoon shade in summer	Medium	Zones 5 to 10	Root rot	Start from transplants in spring or fall; harvest leaves as needed; best flavor in cool weather
Catnip *Nepata cataria*	Aromatic, minty perennial, whose foliage drives cats crazy; dry leaves to make catnip tea to drink or sachet for cats	Warm weather	1 to 2 feet tall, 1 foot wide	Full sun to partial shade	Medium	Zones 4 to 8	None specific	Start from transplants in spring or fall; harvest leaves as needed; keep flowers pinched back
Chives *Allium species* Common chives (lavender flowers), garlic chives (white flowers)	Grasslike perennial with mild onion- or garlic-flavored leaves; pink or white flowers are edible; generally grown for flower or leaves	Cool and warm weather	8 to 16 inches tall, clump-forming	Full sun to partial shade	Medium	Zones 4 to 10	Thrips	Start from transplants in spring or fall; harvest as needed; plant dies back in winter; divide every 2 to 3 years
Cilantro (Coriander) *Coriandrum sativum* Festival, Santo	Tall, lacy-leafed annual with pungent flavor; grown for its foliage to use in ethnic food; edible seeds used in candy and sweets	Cool weather	1 to 2 feet tall, 1 foot wide	Full sun to partial shade	Medium to high	All zones; may overwinter outdoors in Zones 8 to 10	Aphids, whiteflies	Start from plants or seed in early spring or late summer for fall crop; keep flowers pinched back; harvest foliage or let go to seed in summer

HERBS

NAME/SPECIES & SELECTIONS	FEATURES	SEASON	NATURAL SIZE	LIGHT	WATER	RANGE	PESTS/ DISEASES	COMMENTS
Dill *Anethum graveolens* Dill Bouquet, Fernleaf	Tall, airy green annual with delicate fernlike foliage; valued as a salt substitute; edible; yellow flowers	Cool weather	1 to 2 feet tall, 1 foot wide	Full sun to partial shade	Medium to high	All zones; may over-winter outdoors in Zones 8 to 10	Parsley-worm (which becomes the black swal-lowtail butterfly)	Start from transplants (or seed) in early spring or late summer for fall crop; keep flowers pinched back; harvest whole plant before it goes to seed in summer
Fennel *Foeniculum vulgare*	Attractive, Mediter-ranean perennial, with edible, licorice-flavored foliage; green or bronze	Warm weather	1 to 3 feet tall, 1 foot wide	Full sun to partial shade	Medium to high	Zones 6 to 8; may stay evergreen outdoors in Zones 7 to 8	Aphids, parsley-worm	Start from plants or seed in early spring or fall; keep flower heads pinched back; cut back after flowering
Feverfew *Chrysanthemum parthenium*	Ornamental, compact perennial with daisy-like flowers that dry well; once used as medicinal herb	Warm weather	1 to 3 feet tall, equally wide	Full sun or light shade	Medium	Zones 6 to 10	Aphids	Start with transplants in spring or fall; sum-mer flowers dry well
Germander *Teucrium chamaedrys*	Ornamental, old-fashioned evergreen perennial with glossy green leaves; can be sheared as topiary for formal look	All seasons	1 to 2 feet tall, equally wide	Full sun to partial shade	Medium	Zones 5 to 9; must overwinter indoors north of Zone 7	None specific	Start from transplants in spring; use as orna-mental; prune to keep plants in shape; good for accent
Lavender *Lavandula species* ZONE 7 AND NORTH: English lavender ZONES 7 TO 9: French, Provence, Spanish lavenders	Ornamental, fragrant, silvery-leafed ever-green with lavender or pink flowers; sometimes perennial; flowers used to flavor beverages and desserts; scent is popular in perfumes; foliage makes good potpourri	All seasons; flowers in summer	1 to 2 feet tall, equally wide	Full sun	Low to medium	Zones 4 to 9	Root rot	Start from transplants in spring; harvest flowers and foliage as needed; do not wet foliage; keep plants well groomed
Lemon Balm *Melissa officinalis*	Hardy perennial lemon-flavored mint; foliage good for teas, salads, and desserts; thrives from spring to fall; fast grower	Cool and warm weather	1 foot tall, equally wide	Full sun to partial shade	High	Zones 4 to 9	None specific	Start from transplants in early spring or early fall; harvest leaves as needed; prune stems in late summer to stimulate fall growth
Lemon Grass *Cymbopogon citratus*	Tropical, grassy-looking plant with foliage that tastes and smells like lemon; commonly used in Ori-ental cuisine	Warm weather	2 to 3 feet tall, equally wide	Full sun	Medium	All zones; must over-winter indoors in Zone 7 and north	None specific	Start from divisions in spring after last frost; harvest as needed; striking specimen or companion for other lemon-scented herbs
Lemon Verbena *Aloysia triphylla*	Tropical, woody shrub with edible, yellow-green foliage; true lemon scent and fla-vor; delightful in bev-erages, desserts, and salads	Warm weather	2 to 4 feet tall, 1 to 2 feet wide	Full sun	Medium	All zones; must over-winter indoors in Zone 7 and north	None specific	Start from transplants in spring after last frost; harvest leaves as needed

HERBS

NAME/SPECIES & SELECTIONS	FEATURES	SEASON	NATURAL SIZE	LIGHT	WATER	RANGE	PESTS/ DISEASES	COMMENTS
Marjoram *Origanum marjorana* Evergreen marjoram *(O. majoricum),* Sweet marjoram	Low-growing, bushy annual or perennial with small edible leaves; mild oregano flavor; popular in French cooking	Warm weather	1 foot tall, equally wide	Full sun to partial shade	Low to medium	All zones; perennial in pots in Zones 8 to 10	None specific	Start from transplants in spring, 2 weeks after last frost; in Zone 7 and north, harvest entire plant before fall freeze or overwinter inside; use leaves as needed
Mexican Mint Marigold *Tagetes lucida*	Flowering perennial whose foliage tastes like French tarragon; pretty marigold flowers; much easier to grow than tarragon in Lower South; often grown as an annual	Warm weather	2 feet tall, 6 inches wide	Full sun	Medium	Zones 5 to 10	None specific	Start from transplants in spring, 2 weeks after last frost; harvest leaves as tarragon substitute; enjoy flowers for color
Mint *Mentha species* Apple, Chocolate, Orange, Peppermint, Spearmint	Bushy, low-growing perennial foliage plant; prized for its refreshing flavors; evergreen in the Lower South	All seasons	12 to 15 inches tall, spreads indefinitely	Full sun to partial shade	High	Zones 4 to 9; may be evergreen in Lower South	None specific	Start from transplants in spring or fall; harvest foliage as needed; spreads rapidly to fill up pot; tolerates shade; do not let dry out
Oregano *Origanum species* Golden oregano (ornamental), Greek oregano, Italian oregano	Bushy, green-leafed annual or perennial with aromatic foliage and robust flavor; popular in Italian cooking; some selections evergreen in Lower South	All seasons	6 inches to 2 feet tall, equally wide	Full sun to partial shade	Medium	Zones 4 to 10; may be evergreen in Lower South	Aphids, root rot, spider mites	Start from transplants in spring or fall; harvest leaves as needed; easy to grow; spreads rapidly
Parsley *Petroselinum crispum* Curly parsley, French parsley (chervil), Italian parsley	Frilly green biennial/annual with mild peppery taste; great for borders	Cool weather	1 to 2 feet tall, 8 to 12 inches wide	Full sun to partial shade	High	All zones; evergreen in winter in Lower South	Parsley-worm	Start from plants or seed in spring or fall; harvest leaves as needed; keep flowers pinched back to slow plant from setting seed
Rosemary *Rosemarinus officinalis* UPRIGHT: Arp, Salem CREEPING: Mrs. Howard's Creeping, Santa Barbara	Shrubby evergreen annual or perennial; exotic pine scent; tiny blue flowers; creeping form is lovely in hanging baskets; upright form is more cold hardy and can be sheared as topiary	All seasons; flowers late winter through spring	1 to 3 feet tall, equally wide	Full sun	Low to medium	Zones 4 to 8; over-winter indoors in Zone 7 and north	Root rot, spider mites	Start from transplants in spring; harvest as needed (except in winter); prune dead wood each spring; provide good air circulation; grows well once established
Sage *Salvia officinalis* Dwarf sage, Golden sage (ornamental), Purple sage, Tricolor sage	Attractive mounding evergreen perennial, grown for its colorful and aromatic foliage; dwarf or colored selections perform better in Lower South; subject to winter kill in North; often grown as an annual	Warm weather	1 to 1½ feet tall, equally wide	Full sun to partial shade	Medium	Zones 4 to 8	Leaf spot, root rot	Start from transplants in spring or fall; harvest leaves as needed; water base of plant; do not wet foliage or it will spot

HERBS

NAME/SPECIES & SELECTIONS	FEATURES	SEASON	NATURAL SIZE	LIGHT	WATER	RANGE	PESTS/ DISEASES	COMMENTS
Scented Geranium *Pelargonium species* Apple, Coconut, Lemon, Orange, Peppermint, Rose, Strawberry, and other scents/flavors	Tender perennial; fragrant, edible leaves in variety of scents; used to flavor teas, jellies, cakes, and other desserts; small flowers are also edible	Warm weather	1 to 3 feet tall, 1 foot wide	Full sun to partial shade	Low to medium	All zones; must over-winter indoors	Aphids, spider mites, whiteflies	Start from transplants in late spring, 4 weeks after last frost; harvest leaves as needed; bring indoors before fall freeze
Tarragon (French) *Artemisia dracunculus*	Shrubby, upright perennial with aromatic, finely textured green foliage; anise flavor is a classic in French dishes, especially sauces	Cool weather	1 to 2 feet tall, 8 to 12 inches wide	Full sun to partial shade	Medium	Zones 4 to 6; suffers in heat in Zone 7 and south	Powdery mildew, root rot	Start from large transplants in early fall in South; harvest leaves as needed
Thyme *Thymus species* CULINARY: Lemon (*T. citriodous*) ORNAMENTAL: Mother-of-thyme (*T. praecoxarcticus*)	Upright or creeping evergreen perennial, grown for its tiny, savory leaves; popular in cooking; ornamental forms available	All seasons; flowers in spring	4 to 12 inches tall, equally wide	Full sun to partial shade	Low to medium	Zones 4 to 8	Root rot, spider mites	Start from transplants in spring or fall; harvest leaves as needed; do not prune heavily before winter
Winter Savory *Satureja montana*	Low-growing, perennial foliage plant; tiny edible leaves, good for flavoring green beans; evergreen in the Lower South	All seasons	6 to 10 inches tall, spreading to 10 to 20 inches wide	Full sun to partial shade	Medium	Zones 4 to 8	Root rot	Start from transplants in spring or fall; harvest leaves as needed; cut plant back before flowering; do not prune heavily in late fall

VEGETABLES

NAME & SELECTIONS	FEATURES	SEASON	NATURAL SIZE	LIGHT	WATER	RANGE	PESTS/ DISEASES	COMMENTS
Bean, Scarlet Runner (Pink-and-white flowered selections available)	Vining or pole bean; showy scarlet flowers; ornamental, but with edible pods if eaten while young and tender	Warm weather; 50 to 70 days to harvest	5 to 10 feet long, vining or pole	Full sun	High	All zones	Aphids	Start from seed in spring, 2 weeks after last frost; use with trellis or position pot for beans to cover fence or arbor
Bean, Snap BUSH: Blue Lake 274, Contender, Roma II, White Half Runner POLE: Blue Lake FM-1, Kentucky Blue, McCaslan, Rattlesnake	Popular bean for eating; pole/vine or bush types; tender, fleshy pods in green, yellow (wax), or purple; heavy producers	Warm weather; 50 to 70 days to harvest	BUSH: 2 feet tall, equally wide POLE: 5 to 10 feet long, vining or pole	Full sun	High	All zones	Aphids, cucumber beetles, Mexican bean beetles, mildew, whiteflies	Start from seed in spring, 2 weeks after last frost; bush types bear early, but pole types (which need trellis or tepee) are more productive

VEGETABLES

NAME & SELECTIONS	FEATURES	SEASON	NATURAL SIZE	LIGHT	WATER	RANGE	PESTS/ DISEASES	COMMENTS
Beet Action, Burpee Golden, Crosby's Egyptian, Detroit Dark Red, Little Ball, Spinel	Tasty root with tender edible leaves (rich in Vitamin A); comes in several colors, including red, yellow, and white; productive in small space	Cool weather; 45 to 65 days to harvest	8 to 20 inches tall, 8 to 10 inches wide	Full sun	High	All zones	Black spot, leaf miners	Start from seed in early spring, 3 weeks before last frost, or in early fall, 6 to 8 weeks before first frost; be sure to thin seedlings to 4 to 6 inches apart
Broccoli Bonanza, Green Comet, Parkman, Small Miracle	Favorite cole crop for spring or fall; tall, branching vegetable with side branches that produce smaller clusters of green flowerbuds	Cool weather; 60 to 85 days to harvest	1 foot tall, equally wide	Full sun	High	All zones	Cabbage loopers, imported cabbage-worms (fewer pests in fall crops)	Start from transplants in early spring or early fall; harvest anytime after head forms but before florets show yellow
Carrot, Baby Kundulus, Lady Finger, Thumbelina	Baby carrots—1 to 4 inches long—are gourmet delights; fun to grow from seed in soft potting mix	Cool weather; 62 to 70 days to harvest	6 to 8 inches tall, 1 to 2 inches wide	Full sun	High	All zones	Mildew	Start from seed in spring, 2 to 3 weeks before last frost and again in fall, 6 weeks before first frost; be sure to thin to 1 to 2 inches apart
Collard Champion, Georgia, Vates	Traditional cooked green for spring and fall; large, smooth-leafed, cabbagelike plant; cold-hardy; may survive winter in Lower South	Cool weather; 50 to 80 days to harvest	1½ to 3 feet tall, 1 to 2 feet wide	Full sun to partial shade	Medium	All zones	Cabbage loopers, imported cabbage-worms (fewer pests in fall crops)	Start from transplants in early spring or late summer; frost enhances flavor; harvest outside leaves
Cucumber BUSH: Burpless, Lemon Cucumber, Pot Luck, Spacemaster POLE: Sweet Success Hybrid, Suyo Long	Favorite summer salad vegetable; twining vine or bush types available; pretty yellow blooms; green and yellow fruit in variety of shapes and sizes	Warm weather; 50 to 60 days to harvest	BUSH: 2 feet tall, equally wide POLE: 15 feet long, vining or pole	Full sun	High	All zones	Cucumber and flea beetles, spider mites, whiteflies	Start from transplants (or seed) in spring, 2 weeks after last frost; grow vining types on trellis; prune diseased leaves
Eggplant Bambino, Black Beauty, Rosa Bianca, White Beauty	Buttery, mildly sweet, summer vegetable; bush resembles small tree; large, lobed leaves, violet flowers; fruit in many attractive shapes, colors, and sizes	Warm weather; 55 to 85 days to harvest	2 to 3 feet tall, equally wide	Full sun	High	All zones	Aphids, flea beetles, whiteflies	Start from transplants in late spring, 2 to 4 weeks after last frost; cut fruits off vine as soon as they get color to keep plants producing
Gourmet Greens Arugula, Endive, Garden Cress, Radicchio	Grow gourmet greens in spring or fall; use to enhance salads with spicy flavors and colorful foliage	Cool weather; 10 to 90 days to harvest, depending on type	6 inches to 3 feet tall, equally wide	Full sun	Medium	All zones	Aphids, flea beetles, slugs	Start from transplants in spring, 2 weeks before last frost, or start in late summer for fall crop; cover in case of frost; use to enliven purchased greens

VEGETABLES

NAME & SELECTIONS	FEATURES	SEASON	NATURAL SIZE	LIGHT	WATER	RANGE	PESTS/ DISEASES	COMMENTS
Kale Dwarf Blue Curled, Dwarf Siberian, Vates	Traditional cooked green for spring and fall; large, curly leaves; resembles parsley, but bigger and thicker; may survive winter in Lower South	Cool weather; 55 to 75 days to harvest	1½ to 3 feet tall, 1 to 2 feet wide	Full sun	Medium	All zones	Cabbage loopers, imported cabbage-worms (fewer pests in fall crops)	Start from transplants in early spring or late summer; frost enhances flavor; harvest outer leaves
Lettuce LOOSELEAF: Bibb, Black-Seeded Simpson, Butter-crunch, Mignonette, Red Oak Leaf, Red Sails, Tom Thumb ROMAINE: Dark Green Cos, Parris Island, White Paris	Favorite salad crop for spring and fall; various shades of green and red; looseleaf and romaine types easier to grow than California-type head lettuce; may survive mild winter; as ornamental as it is edible; mesclun mixes feature a variety of young, small salad greens	Cool weather; 45 to 65 days to harvest	6 to 12 inches tall, 6 to 18 inches wide	Full sun	Medium	All zones	Aphids	Start from seed or transplants, 2 weeks before last frost (but cover if frost threat-ens), or set out in late summer for fall crop; harvest outside leaves; use to enliven salads with purchased lettuce
Onions, Bunching (Scallions) Evergreen, Hardy White, Ishikuro, Iwatsuki, White Lisbon, White Spear	Savory addition to meals in spring and fall; bunching or green onions make small bulbs grown for their mild-tasting foliage; bulbs may be peren-nial in Lower South	Cool weather; 45 to 60 days to harvest	8 to 10 inches tall, 1 to 2 inches wide	Full sun to partial shade	High	All zones	Thrips	Start onions from transplants in early spring or early fall; harvest stems as needed; harvest entire plant before hard freeze
Peas, Edible-Podded SNOW PEAS: Snowbird SUGAR SNAPS: Dwarf Gray Sugar, Sugar Bon, Sugar Daddy	Easier to grow than English peas, these vegetables are spring and summer favorites; both pods and peas are edible; peas are delicious freshly picked	Cool weather; 60 to 75 days to harvest	BUSH: 1 to 3 feet tall, equally wide VINE: 6 feet long	Full sun	High	All zones	Downy mildew, powdery mildew, spider mites	Start from seed in early spring or late summer; use trellis with vining selections; water at base of plant to avoid wetting foliage and inviting mildew
Peppers BELL: Better Belle, Lemon Belle, Orange Belle, Red Beauty HOT: Habañero, Hungarian Yellow Wax, Jalepeño SWEET: Gypsy, Red Cherry, Sweet Banana	Classic multipurpose summer vegetable; compact, shrublike plants with colorful fruit in many shapes and sizes; produces continually, summer to fall	Warm weather; 55 to 75 days to harvest	1 to 3 feet tall, 1 to 2 feet wide	Full sun	High	All zones	Aphids, Colorado potato beetles, whiteflies	Start from transplants in late spring, 2 to 4 weeks after last frost; stake plants to prevent them from falling over
Potato Anoka, Caribe, Irish Cobbler, Kennebec, Red Pontiac	Satisfying spring or fall crop; compact plants; variety of types and colors; fun for children to grow in containers; choose heat-tolerant selections	Cool weather; 60 to 90 days to harvest	18 inches tall, equally wide	Full sun to partial shade	High	All zones	Blister beetles, Colorado potato beetles, flea beetles	Start in early spring or fall from minitubers (or seed potatoes); add loose soil as plant grows, do not cover stems completely; dig new potatoes when tops flower, dig mature potatoes when tops die down

VEGETABLES

NAME & SELECTIONS	FEATURES	SEASON	NATURAL SIZE	LIGHT	WATER	RANGE	PESTS/ DISEASES	COMMENTS
Spinach FALL OR SPRING: Bloomsdale Long Standing FALL: Chesapeake, Dixie Market SPRING: Avon, Estivato	Classic spring and fall green for salad or cooking; easy to grow; flavor sweetened by frost; productive, fast grower	Cool weather; 35 to 70 days to harvest	6 to 10 inches tall, 6 to 8 inches wide	Full sun	High	All zones	Flea beetles, leaf miners	Start from transplants in early fall or early spring; harvest outside leaves or entire clump; tolerates freezing weather but goes to seed in summer
Squash, Summer SCALLOP: Pattypan, Peter Pan, Sunburst YELLOW SQUASH: Butterbar, Early Golden Summer ZUCCHINI: Gourmet Globe	Colorful summer stir-fry vegetable; bush and vining types; fruit comes in variety of colors, shapes, and sizes; long bearing; yellow flowers are edible	Warm weather; 35 to 60 days to harvest	BUSH: 2 to 3 feet tall, 2 to 4 feet wide VINE: 2 to 4 feet tall	Full sun	High	All zones	Cucumber beetles, powdery mildew, squash bugs, squash vine borers	Start from transplants (or seed) in spring right after last frost; control pests; remove diseased foliage; pick when fruit is 4 to 6 inches, or harvest "baby" squash early
Sweet Potato CULINARY: Bush Porto Rico (Vineless), Vardaman ORNAMENTAL: Blackie, Margarita, Sulfur	Old-fashioned summer favorite; vitamin-rich tubers thrive during long summers; easy to grow; attractive foliage; also grown as ornamental vines in hanging baskets, as trailers, or on arbors	Warm weather; 100 to 120 days to harvest	1 to 2 feet tall, equally wide or vining	Full sun	Medium	All zones	Beetles, sweet potato weevils	Start from certified disease-free slips in spring, 3 weeks after last frost; do not use high-nitrogen fertilizer; harvest before first frost
Swiss Chard Fordhook Giant, Geneva, Lucullus Light Green, Rhubarb	Form of beet grown for leaves and stalks; popular as cooked green; tall with striking foliage; ornamental and heat tolerant; red- and white-stemmed selections; produces from spring to fall	Warm and cool weather; 55 to 60 days to harvest	2 feet tall, 1½ feet wide	Full sun	High	All zones	None specific	Start from transplants (or seed) from early spring to late summer; easy to grow; harvest outside leaves as new leaves grow in center
Tomato LARGE FRUIT: Better Bush, Celebrity, Patio SMALL FRUIT: Roma, Small Fry, Sweet 100, Tiny Tim, Yellow Pear	Most popular home-grown vegetable; cherry tomatoes are easiest for containers, but some larger tomatoes have been adapted to pots, including both bush and vining types	Warm weather; 65 to 80 days to harvest	BUSH: 3 to 4 feet tall, 1 to 2 feet wide VINE: 3 to 8 feet long	Full sun	High	All zones	Blossom end rot (calcium deficiency brought on by drought), leaf spot, spider mites, wilt	Start from transplants in spring, 2 weeks after last frost; plant deep so lowest leaves are just above soil level; mulch, stake, or trellis plants; watch for pests; do not allow soil to dry out; pick fruit regularly

Trees and Shrubs

A matched pair of evergreen trees in containers carries the lush green of this landscape right up to the doorway.

Trees and shrubs bring evergreen foliage to a bare corner, fragrance to a patio, and seasonal displays of spring flowers, autumn foliage, or bright berries to a small courtyard. Because they are generally long-lasting features and do not require replanting often, most trees and shrubs in containers involve less daily care than flowers or seasonal plants. Once in place, they become an integral part of the landscape design, requiring you to make only occasional changes to their arrangement.

Because of their size, containerized trees and shrubs have greater presence in a garden than do smaller potted plants.

Designing with Trees and Shrubs

Whether it's a lacy Japanese maple displayed in the center of a small courtyard or a pair of boxwoods accenting a doorway, a woody ornamental plant in a pot lends an established look to any garden.

A pine tree in a container softens the angular lines of the arbor and the patio.

The perfect rosette of sago palm is like a living sculpture.

Trees in Containers

A potted tree catches the eye and is ideal for directing attention. For example, a formal entryway accented by two Little Gem magnolias in large classical pots is as grand as when the trees are planted in the ground. In containers, trees add vertical interest and character to flat places around the house and the garden, such as a porch, a patio, a pool area, or a deck. Also, trees in pots, like trees in the ground, offer welcome shade and make appealing specimens.

It is important to choose the right tree for the location and for the purpose you have in mind. Here are a few questions to help you in your selection: Do you want a plant the size of an evergreen or deciduous tree? Are you looking for spring or summer flowers, for fall leaf color, for berries, or for all three? Does the tree you are considering prefer sunlight or shade? Is the tree neat, or does it drop leaves, seeds, or fruit? What is the final expected size of the tree in a container?

Small trees—10 to 15 feet in height—are generally the best candidates for containers, as their flowers, foliage, and fruit remain within easy reach. (Shrubs can also be limbed up to resemble small trees.) Trees look dramatic in pots but, after a short period, grow more slowly than they would if in the ground. A tree that grows to 30 feet in the ground may reach only 10 to 15 feet in a container. In addition, the tree can be kept smaller through pruning.

Each tree mentioned in the chart on pages 105 and 106 brings something unique to the garden when grown in a container. For year-round interest, try an elegant flowering evergreen, such as Little Gem magnolia; a soft conifer, such as Leyland cypress; or a hardy native evergreen that covers itself with berries, such as holly. Some trees are exceptional for their seasonal interest. Consider deciduous trees with appealing fall color, branching, or bark, such as Japanese maple; or choose a tree that flowers at a specific time, such as spring-blooming star magnolia or summer-blooming crepe myrtle.

Caladiums and a trailing spider plant add seasonal color and texture to this Little Gem magnolia.

FILLING IN UNDER THE TRUNKS

Some trees and shrubs, such as crepe myrtle, wax myrtle, and yaupon holly, have open, leggy trunks with handsome markings or interesting form. To fill the open space near the trunks, set out a mixture of smaller plants around the base of the tree or the shrub. Variegated plants, complementary flowers, and foliage plants in different textures and shades of green and blue all add light to otherwise evergreen plantings. Use houseplants to fill in gaps during the summer or plant a permanent ground cover, such as liriope.

Primroses set at the foot of this Japanese maple help maintain color even when the tree is leafless.

An evergreen native shrub with a natural arching form, leucothoe is a perfect addition to any shady area. The foliage keeps its color long after being cut and is frequently used in arrangements.

Shrubs in Containers

Since shrubs come in so many different sizes and forms, the options are endless for using shrubs in containers. Potted shrubs highlight the changing seasons in a garden yet add a sense of permanence. An evergreen Japanese andromeda, with its dainty spring blooms and striking new foliage, is an excellent choice for enlivening a shady entryway. A sprawling, old-fashioned flowering deutzia puts on a brilliant spring show on a sunny patio. Even as common a plant as nandina makes a dramatic statement in a container, with its winter foliage color and bright red berries. A potted juniper can double as a holiday arrangement and, accented with annuals in season, a spring-to-fall display. Most shrubs in pots are small enough to be moved easily into the background as soon as their seasonal shows are over.

When selecting a shrub for a container, follow the same guidelines as you would for choosing a tree. Consider the shrub's seasonal features and horticultural needs, along with the maintenance required. For example, some shrubs, such as boxwood, camellia, and

Old-fashioned deutzia in a large container makes a lovely springtime accent. When the flowers fade, add pots of summer annuals, such as geraniums or petunias, to the foreground.

Japanese andromeda, take several years to reach the desired height; therefore, buying a large specimen might be a good idea. Others, such as deuztia, leucothoe, and nandina, grow faster, perhaps needing occasional pruning to keep them in bounds. To economize, purchase small sizes of these shrubs and let them grow into their space. Remember, too, that some shrubs, such as ligustrum and privet, can be limbed up or pruned so that they take on a treelike form. And you can trim the colorful cotoneaster or the flowering camellia, among others, to resemble a topiary.

Flowing ivy fills in the base of a free-form cotoneaster. (A layer of gravel was added inside the container to keep the planting from toppling in the wind.)

Growing Trees and Shrubs in Containers

With the right care, a tree or a shrub will survive in a container for an average of three to five years before repotting is required. (See pages 55 and 56 for information on repotting.) When first planting, make certain to choose the proper container and good soil. Also, be sure that the drainage is excellent, and you may need to add bottom weight to counterbalance the plant's top growth.

Choosing Containers for Trees and Shrubs

There are special considerations to take into account when selecting containers for trees and shrubs. Naturally, the larger the tree or the shrub, the larger the container required. The pot must accommodate the root ball and be stable enough to anchor the plant. This usually means a 10-gallon (or larger) container that is at least 18 inches wide and 24 inches deep. As a rule, the pot should be 5 inches wider in diameter than the root ball (or the nursery pot); wooden barrels, tubs, or planters are ideal. Keep in mind that trees or shrubs will grow larger in larger containers. If you want your new tree to eventually cast some shade on a deck or a patio, plant it in a pot that measures about 3 feet tall and is equally wide.

Since the tree or the shrub will be a permanent planting, choose a container made of weatherproof materials that will withstand winter freezing and thawing. (See pages 26–29 for more information on weatherproof pots.) If your heart is set on a decorative container that is not weatherproof, leave the plant in its nursery pot and use the other as a cachepot.

Planting Trees and Shrubs in Containers

To lessen the shock of moving, plant trees and shrubs in the fall or early spring, while they are dormant. This allows time for the plants to get settled in before summer heat begins. A pot is usually heavy after it has been filled with soil and plant material, so plant the container at the selected site.

When preparing the containers, cover the drainage hole with coarse screen so that the soil and the roots will stay in the pot. Then add a layer of gravel to balance the plant's top growth and to keep the pot from tipping over in the wind. In the case of particularly windy sites, such as balconies and rooftops, fill the pot almost a third full with gravel.

When choosing a pot for a shrub, be sure the pot is large enough to hold the root ball (with room to spare) but not so large that the shrub is overpowered. This neat boxwood and medium-sized concrete planter complement each other beautifully.

Most upright trees and shrubs, particularly topiaries, are likely to be top-heavy. They need a heavier potting soil than flowers. Ivy and geraniums fill in the base of this boxwood.

Selecting a Potting Soil

Be sure to use a potting mix made especially for trees and shrubs. This soil needs to be heavier than that of potting mix made for flowers and smaller plants; the increase in weight of the soil ensures the stability of top-heavy trees and shrubs. The slightly denser soil mix, which often contains composted bark instead of sphagnum peat moss, also helps prevent trees and shrubs from drying out quickly in direct sunlight. At planting, remember to mix a controlled-release tree-and-shrub fertilizer, such as 12-6-6, into the potting mix (if one was not already added).

How to Plant

Gently remove the plant from its container and untangle the matted root ball. If the plant is root bound, make a cut in the bottom of the root ball and loosen the roots. If you're planting a balled-and-burlapped tree or shrub in a container, gently pull the fabric back from the top, keeping the root ball intact. Place the tree or the shrub into the new pot so that the top of the root ball is within 2 inches of the rim. Fill in with moistened potting mix and level off the mix to within ½ to 1 inch of the rim. You may fold or cut the fabric away. If necessary, after watering, firm the surface with your fingers. Do not fill the pot too full, or the soil will wash out when you water.

After planting, give the tree or the shrub a thorough watering. Add a ½-inch layer of mulch to help keep roots moist and cool in the summer. If the tree or the shrub is top-heavy when first planted, add a supporting stake. Place the stake in the container (avoid the root ball) and tie it loosely to the plant.

GOOD COMPANIONS FOR POTTED TREES AND SHRUBS

These plants are excellent fillers for the base of a pot containing a tree or a large tree-form shrub.

Annuals and bulbs: Caladiums, daffodils, geraniums, impatiens, Japanese roof iris, pansies, primrose, and wax begonias.

Trailers: Carolina jessamine, lantana, ornamental sweet potato vine, periwinkle, petunia (trailing types), variegated English ivy, and verbena (trailing types).

Herbs and vegetables: Creeping thyme, golden oregano, marjoram, prostrate rosemary, and red lettuce.

Ferns: Autumn fern, holly fern, Japanese painted fern, and maidenhair fern.

Ground covers and grasses: Ajuga, carex, hosta, liriope, and mondo.

Houseplants: Asparagus fern, pothos, spider plant, Swedish ivy, and wandering Jew.

Care and Maintenance

Trees and shrubs in containers need regular watering. The amount of water needed varies with each selection. For example, junipers require light watering, but camellias must have consistently damp soil. Generally, trees and shrubs need to be watered more frequently when they are planted in porous containers (such as clay) and placed in direct sunlight or when they are situated under a roof or an awning where rain cannot reach them.

It's difficult to set a watering schedule for trees and shrubs; each individual plant has its own requirements, depending on the selection, its growth habits, the type of container, where the container is located, and the potting soil used. Most plants suffer in soggy soil, so do not overwater them. Get in the habit of testing the soil with your index finger; water whenever the soil is dry to a depth of 2 to 3 inches. A tree or a shrub will require more water the longer it remains in a container; plants in pots slowly become root bound as there is not enough soil to hold moisture for the roots.

Twice a year—early in the spring and summer—scratch a controlled-release tree-and-shrub fertilizer, such as 12-6-6, into the soil. If the plant has already reached the desired height, cut back fertilizing to once a year.

Many of these trees will outgrow their containers in a year or so. Plant the tree in the ground elsewhere in your landscape or give it to a school, a library, or a community organization.

Get to know your plants' individual watering needs. Conifers, such as this blue juniper, require less water than do many deciduous trees and shrubs.

TREES

NAME/ SELECTIONS	FEATURES	SEASON	NATURAL SIZE	LIGHT	WATER	RANGE	PESTS/ DISEASES	COMMENTS
Crepe Myrtle *Lagerstroemia indica* MILDEW-RESISTANT SELECTIONS: Catawba, Natchez, Powhatan, Seminole	Deciduous; exquisite bark and flowers; vase-shaped; rapid grower	Summer, winter	3 to 25 feet tall, 15 to 25 foot spread	Full sun; trees in shade will not bloom well	Medium to high	Zones 7 to 9	Aphids, powdery mildew, sooty mold	Plant in spring; tip-prune in late summer and late winter to shape and to promote flowering
Curly Filbert (Harry Lauder's Walking Stick) *Corylus avellana* Contorta	Deciduous; curled and twisted stems; slow to moderate grower	Winter	8 to 10 feet tall, 4 to 6 foot spread	Full sun to partial shade	Medium	Zones 4 to 8	Blight	Plant in spring or fall; prune to maintain size and to shape; use as specimen
Cutleaf Sumac (Staghorn) *Rhus typhina* Dissecta, Laciniata	Native, deciduous; yellow to scarlet leaves in fall; upright, spreading form; rapid grower	Fall, winter	15 feet tall, equal or greater spread	Full sun	Low to medium	Zones 3 to 8	None specific	Plant in spring or fall; bears clusters of crimson fruit in winter; prune in late winter to maintain size
Dwarf Alberta Spruce *Picea glauca* Conica	Native of Canada, evergreen; compact, conical form; light to gray-green foliage; slow grower	All seasons	7 feet tall, 2 to 4 foot spread	Full sun	Medium to high	Zones 2 to 7	Bagworm; mites; spruce, root, and trunk rot	Plant in spring or fall; prune to maintain shape; popular holiday tree; good natural formal shape
Hinoki False Cypress *Chamaecyparis obtusa* Filifera Aurea, Gracilis, Nana Gracilis	Evergreen; slender upright form with nodding branches; dwarf, golden, and variegated forms available; slow grower	All seasons	4 to 20 feet tall, 2 to 6 foot spread	Full sun	Medium to high	Zones 4 to 8	None specific	Plant in spring or fall; prune to maintain shape; good as containerized hedge
Japanese Maple *Acer palmatum* Many selections based on leaf color, size, and shape	Deciduous; airy, delicate foliage, sculptural form; slow grower; dwarf types grow to less than 6 feet tall	All seasons	6 to 15 feet tall, equal spread	Full sun to partial shade	Medium to high	Zones 5 to 8	Aphids	Plant in spring or fall; prune to accent horizontal form; use as accent or specimen
Leyland Cypress *Cupressocyparis leylandii*	Evergreen; conifer, formal, or pyramidal shape; fast grower	All seasons	50 to 60 feet tall, 10 to 15 foot spread	Full sun	Medium to high	Zones 6 to 10	Bagworm, canker	Plant in spring or fall; prune for size and shape; good screen or holiday tree
Mugho Pine *Pinus mugo* Compacta, Mugo, Pumilio	Evergreen; shrubby, symmetrical form; slow grower	All seasons	4 feet tall, 2 to 3 foot spread	Full sun	Medium to high	Zones 2 to 7	Borers, rust, scale, wood rot	Plant in spring or fall; pick plants with dense, pleasing form; good specimen
River Birch *Betula nigra* Heritage	Native, deciduous; outstanding bark; provides winter show; attractive, multi-stemmed trunk; rapid grower	Summer, winter	40 to 70 feet tall, 40 to 60 foot spread	Full sun	Medium to high	Zones 4 to 9	Aphids	Plant in spring or fall; likes acid soil mix; best birch for South

TREES

NAME/ SELECTIONS	FEATURES	SEASON	NATURAL SIZE	LIGHT	WATER	RANGE	PESTS/ DISEASES	COMMENTS
Southern Magnolia *Magnolia grandiflora* Edith Bogue, Little Gem, Symmes Select	Native, evergreen; large, glossy leaves; dense foliage with fragrant white blooms; slender, upright form; slow grower	All seasons; blooms in spring	20 feet tall, 10 foot spread	Full sun to partial shade	Medium to high	Zones 7 to 9	Chlorosis	Plant in spring or fall; prune to shape; useful for screen, accent, or formal settings
Spruce Pine *Pinus glabra*	Native, evergreen; broad, open dark green needles; slow grower	All seasons	15 to 40 feet tall, 10 to 30 foot spread	Full sun	Medium to high	Zones 4 to 8	None specific	Plant in spring or fall; prune to maintain shape; good as specimen or screen
Star Magnolia *Magnolia stellata* Royal Star, Waterlily* *Select late bloomers to avoid frost	Deciduous; lovely white, star-shaped blooms; upright, spreading form; slow grower	Spring	1 to 10 feet tall, 15 to 20 foot spread	Full sun to partial shade	Medium to high	Zones 4 to 8	None specific	Plant in fall; prune after blooming to maintain shape; enjoy as specimen or accent
Yaupon Holly *Ilex vomitoria* Weeping selections are striking	Native, evergreen; tiny leaves and clear red berries in fall; upright, spreading form; moderate grower	Fall and winter	15 to 20 feet tall, 5 to 8 foot spread	Full sun	Low to medium	Zones 7 to 10	None specific	Plant in spring or fall; prune for size and shape; good as topiary

SHRUBS

NAME/SPECIES & SELECTIONS	FEATURES	SEASON	NATURAL SIZE	LIGHT	WATER	RANGE	PESTS/ DISEASES	COMMENTS
Chinese Holly *Ilex cornuta* Berries Jubilee, Dazzler, Dwarf Burford, Willow Leaf	Evergreen; dense or open form; glossy, spiny leaves and large, red or yellow long-lasting berries; all selections set fruit without pollination	All seasons	3 to 10 feet tall, 3 to 6 feet wide	Full sun to partial shade (full sun produces more berries)	Low to medium	Zones 7 to 9	Leaf miner, scale, spider mites	Plant in fall or early spring; heat and drought tolerant; attracts birds; good as accent or hedge
Chinese Juniper *Juniperus chinensis* Blue Pfitzer, Blue Point, Blue Vase, Torulosa	Evergreen; broadly columnar; dense needle foliage; slow to moderate grower	All seasons	7 to 8 feet tall, 3 feet wide, columnar	Full sun	Medium	Zones 6 to 10	Bagworm, blight, borer, rust, scale, webworm	Plant in spring or fall; prune to maintain size and shape; can be shaped as topiary; good for accent or screen
Common Boxwood *Buxus sempervirens*	Evergreen; dense, stately form and small, glossy leaves; Southern garden classic; slow grower	All seasons	3 to 15 feet tall, equally wide	Full sun or shade	Medium to high	Zones 5 to 8	Leaf miner, root rot	Plant in fall or early spring; pair in containers makes elegant accent; can be shaped as topiary

SHRUBS

NAME/SPECIES & SELECTIONS	FEATURES	SEASON	NATURAL SIZE	LIGHT	WATER	RANGE	PESTS/ DISEASES	COMMENTS
Common Camellia *Camellia japonica* Sasanqua camellia *(C. sasanqua)*	Evergreen; dense upright form and large, glossy dark green leaves, exquisite white, pink, red, lavender, and striped flowers; Southern garden classic; slow grower	All seasons; common camellia blooms in late winter, sasanqua camellia blooms in fall	6 to 12 feet tall, 3 to 6 feet wide	Partial shade	Medium to high	Zones 7 to 9	Chlorosis, tea scale	Plant in fall, winter, or early spring; provides brilliant winter color; choose cold-hardy camellias for Zone 7; grow in standard pot or espalier
Cotoneaster *Cotoneaster species* LOW-SPREADING: Bearberry cotoneaster *(C. dammeri),* Rock cotoneaster *(C. horozontalis)* UPRIGHT: Willowleaf cotoneaster *(C. salicifolius)*	Evergreen; upright or curving branches (depending on species) and tiny dark green leaves; bears shiny orange-red fruit that attracts birds	All seasons; has small whitish flowers in spring, berries in early fall	1 to 10 feet tall, 3 to 6 feet wide	Full sun to light shade	Medium	Zones 4 to 8	Cotoneaster webworm, fireblight, lacebugs, spider mites	Plant in fall or early spring; allow large selections to keep natural shape; prune old wood and bent branches each year
Deutzia *Deutzia species* and hybrids Godsall Pink, Nikko, Pride of Rochester	Deciduous; masses of showy white to purple spring flowers; some flowers fragrant; old-fashioned	Spring	1 to 10 feet tall, up to 5 feet wide	Full sun to partial shade	Medium to high	Zones 6 to 10	None specific	Plant in fall or early spring; prune after flowering, cut oldest stems to ground every other year; place in front of evergreen background
Japanese Andromeda *Pieris japonica* Compacta, Mountain Fire, Variegata	Evergreen; upright, twisting form; whorled, glossy leaves with delicate pearl-like flowers in late winter to spring; new growth is red; slow grower	All seasons	3 to 9 feet tall, 2 to 4 feet wide	Partial shade	Medium to high	Zones 5 to 8	Chlorosis, lacebugs, root rot	Plant in fall or early spring; shelter from wind; excellent specimen tree with year-round good looks
Japanese Cleyera *Cleyera japonica* Tricolor *(C. Fortuna),* Variegata	Evergreen; upright, arching branches and large, glossy dark green leaves; moderate grower	All seasons	8 to 10 feet tall, 5 to 6 feet wide	Partial shade	Medium to high	Zones 7 to 9	None specific	Plant in spring or summer; shelter from winter cold in Zone 7; good accent; shape by pruning
Japanese Yew *Taxus cuspidata* Captiva, Nigra	Evergreen; conifer, compact, or pyramidal form; slow grower	All seasons	3 to 15 feet tall, equal or greater spread	Full sun to shade	Medium	Zones 4 to 7	None specific	Plant in spring or fall; prune to maintain shape; good for formal settings or topiary
Leucothoe *Leucothoe fontanesiana* Lovita, Scarletta Coastal leucothoe *(L. axillaris),* Sweetbells *(L. racemosa)*	Native, evergreen; graceful, arching form; leathery, lime green leaves and clusters of tiny, urn-shaped flowers in spring; foliage can turn bronzy	All seasons; flowers in spring	2 to 8 feet tall, equally wide	Partial to full shade	Medium to high	Zones 6 to 10	Leaf spot	Plant in fall or early spring; prune lightly; use in groups or as hedge; foliage is long-lasting in arrangements

SHRUBS

NAME/SPECIES & SELECTIONS	FEATURES	SEASON	NATURAL SIZE	LIGHT	WATER	RANGE	PESTS/ DISEASES	COMMENTS
Ligustrum *Ligustrum japonicum* Howard, Rotundifolium, Variegatum	Evergreen; glossy dark green or variegated foliage; white flower spikes; produces berries that attract birds; fast grower	All seasons; flowers in late spring, produces berries in fall	6 to 18 feet tall, 6 to 8 feet wide	Full sun	Medium	Zones 7 to 10	None specific	Plant in fall or early spring; shrubs can be limbed up to tree forms, pruned formally, or shaped as topiary
Nandina (Heavenly Bamboo) *Nandina domestica* Alba (white), Compacta, Harbour Dwarf, Purpurea	Evergreen; upright canes, delicate foliage that turns burnished red or white in fall; produces lots of berries that attract birds; provides lovely color for winter arrangements	All seasons; flowers in spring, makes berries in winter	1 to 8 feet tall, 3 to 4 feet wide	Full sun to shade	Medium	Zones 6 to 9	None specific	Plant anytime; group at least 3 plants together to ensure berry production; dwarf selections available, but they may not produce berries; maintain natural look by pruning each stalk a different height
Needle Palm *Rhapidophyllum hystrix*	Native, shrubby palm from Coastal Plains; arching stems of lustrous, dark green leaf fans; possibly hardiest palm in existence; slow grower	All seasons	6 to 8 feet tall, equally wide	Full sun to shade	Medium to high	Zones 6 to 10	None specific	Plant in fall, spring, or summer; good accent plant or filler in border; buy from catalogues or nurseries specializing in native plants; do not dig from the wild
Pittosporum *Pittosporum tobira*	Evergreen; crisp, dense foliage, neat form; thick leaves whorled at ends; tiny fragrant flowers; steady, sprawling growth	All seasons	3 to 10 feet tall, 4 to 15 feet wide	Full sun to shade, protect from severe winds, especially in winter	Low to medium	Zones 8 to 10	None specific; lightly prune branches damaged by cold	Plant in late spring; sturdy, neat evergreen for hot climates and beach; use as accent, screen, or anchor in border
Pyracantha (Firethorn) *Pyracantha species* and hybrids DISEASE-RESISTANT HYBRIDS: Apache, Fiery Cascade, Teton, Tiny Tim, Yukon Belle	Evergreen; erratic branching and tiny leaves; features clusters of white flowers, thorns, and tons of red or orange berries; look for smaller, less thorny hybrids; fast grower	All seasons; flowers in midspring, provides berries in fall	6 to 18 feet tall, equally wide	Full sun	Low to medium	Zones 6 to 9	Aphids, fireblight, scab on fruit, scale; choose disease-resistant types	Plant in spring, summer, or fall; prune to control size, to create garland, or to espalier
Wax Myrtle *Myrica cerifera*	Native, evergreen; upright form and small, glossy, aromatic leaves; female's grayish white fruit used by pioneers to make candles; rapid grower	All seasons	10 to 20 feet tall, 15 to 20 feet wide	Full sun to partial shade	Low to medium	Zones 7 to 9	None specific	Plant in spring or fall; can be limbed up as a tree form; use as specimen on deck or patio, as corner accent, or as screen; good plant for beach
Yucca *Yucca species* Adam's Needle (*Y. filamentosa*), Bear Grass (*Y. smalliana*)	Native, evergreen shrubs or small trees; tough, sword-shaped leaves; large clusters of white or yellow flowers; old-fashioned	All seasons; blooms in summer	SHRUBS: leaves 1 to 3 feet long and wide, flower spikes 2 to 15 feet tall SMALL TREES: 7 to 12 feet tall, 2 to 3 feet wide	Full sun	Low to medium	Zones 7 to 10	None specific	Plant in fall, spring, or summer; taller kinds make striking specimens or vertical accents; locate plants with sharp leaves out of traffic patterns

Roses

Caring for roses is often easier when you grow them in pots rather than in the ground.

Growing roses successfully in containers depends on selecting types best adapted to pots and paying careful attention to the plants' particular needs. Ground cover roses, miniatures, tree roses, polyanthas, and other roses that grow only 3 or 4 feet or less adapt well to sizable planters. Large-flowered modern climbers (but not ramblers) can be planted in half-barrel containers for training on a trellis or over an archway. Small cascading roses thrive in hanging baskets, provided the containers are of sufficient size.

A tree rose makes an elegant vertical accent for an entryway.

When given the sun they need, potted roses flower as well as those planted in the ground.

Growing Roses in Containers

Roses need plenty of sunlight to bloom well. They require four to eight hours of full sunlight and so are ideal for sunny decks, walkways, and patios. Some roses will bloom (less prolifically) if given bright morning sun or dappled sunlight all day. Planting roses in containers allows you to move the plants around until you find just the right spot for display or the most sunlight for maximum bloom.

There are many types and forms of roses. Spreading ground cover roses, such as Flower Carpet, are perfect for window boxes and hanging baskets. Polyanthas and other low-growing roses in pots make handsome accent or specimen plants. Miniatures in containers brighten a patio or create a line of color across the railing of a deck or a balcony.

Tree roses often are grown in pots for greater impact. Large modern roses planted in containers do not sprawl, unlike plants grown in the ground—an advantage for gardeners with limited space. Climbing roses present a bit of a challenge. Extensive runners mean an extensive root system is needed to support this growth; therefore, these plants require oversize containers—at least 2 feet wide and 2 feet deep.

Roses look stark in the winter when all that's visible are the plants' leafless canes. However, since large roses are placed in large pots, there is plenty of room for underplantings of trailing plants, evergreen ground covers, and cool-weather annuals that add interest and divert attention from the bare canes.

Decide which size rose best fits the chosen space; consider the style of rose as well—for example, thorny selections are only for low-traffic areas. Choose from the toughest locally adapted, disease-resistant selections. Buying plants in bloom allows you to see the colors of selections. (See the chart on page 114 for just a few roses suitable for growing in containers. Most types of roses adapt well to a wide variety of growing conditions, so feel free to choose from the vast number of available selections.)

Choosing Containers for Roses

To grow well, roses must have ample room to spread, which is why pot size is critical to success. For miniatures, polyanthas, and other roses less than 4 feet tall, choose containers at least 14 to 16 inches in diameter and of equal or greater depth. Larger climbers, floribundas, and hybrid teas need containers at least 16 inches in diameter and 16 to 18 inches deep; wooden half-barrels and oversize planters are good containers for these roses.

Terra-cotta, concrete, or wooden pots are ideal for roses because they are porous and help keep the soil from becoming waterlogged. You may use plastic containers, but proper drainage is a must. Plastic pots are lighter than concrete, wooden, or terra-cotta containers and retain moisture longer during periods of drought.

All containers must have one or more drainage holes to keep the potting medium from becoming supersaturated when overwatered or during heavy periods of rain. (See pages 24–33 for more information about choosing containers.)

Choosing a Potting Soil

There are potting mixes specifically formulated for roses. These mixes tend to be heavier than potting mixes for other flowers and smaller plants, to better anchor the roots and to ensure stability. You might prefer to make your own mix.

Blend equal parts of a quality spaghnum peat-based potting mix with well-composted bark. Composted bark retains moisture longer than does peat moss, provides more stability in light winds, and is less expensive. Some gardeners even add two parts soil to two parts bark and one part sand, but the soil must be free of insects or diseases. This slightly denser soil mix is appropriate for containerized roses in direct sunlight because it prevents them from drying out quickly. At planting, mix a controlled-release rose fertilizer into the potting soil.

The key to growing roses in pots is selecting plants that thrive in containers, such as this miniature rose. A deep urn allows plenty of room for the roots.

Planted and staked while still leafless in late winter, a tree rose will fill out and be laden with blooms by late spring.

Planting Roses in Pots

Roses are best transplanted in late winter or early spring, while they are dormant or semidormant. This lessens transplant shock and gives the roses time to settle in before the summer heat begins. However, many gardeners wait until later in the spring to buy because that is when the roses begin to bloom. Spring-planted roses need more regular watering than those planted earlier.

Pots can be heavy after they are full of soil, so move your containers to the selected site before you plant. To prepare a pot, cover the drainage hole with coarse screen so that soil and roots do not leave the pot. If planting a climber or a tree rose, add a layer of gravel to keep the pot from tipping over. At particularly windy sites, such as balconies or terraces, fill a third of the pot with gravel. Add moistened potting mix until the pot is about three-quarters full.

Gently remove the plant from the container. Untangle any roots that are matted. Place the rose in the new pot with the surface of the root ball within about 2 inches of the rim. Fill in around the sides of the root ball with potting mix, firming the surface of the medium with your fingers. Level off the mix within about 1 inch of the rim. Be sure not to fill the pot too full (or the soil will wash out when you water) and do not set the root ball too high in the container. Soak by watering the pot three times.

If planting a bare-root rose, form a small mound of soil in the bottom of the pot and then place the rose in the container, fanning the roots out in a circle to cover the mound. Add soil around the roots and then fill the pot with mix up to the **crown** (where roots meet the stem). The crown of the rose should be 1 to 2 inches below the rim. Water thoroughly three times to settle the soil.

Mulch with a 1- to 2-inch layer of compost, straw, pine bark, or similar material to conserve moisture and to prevent weeds from germinating in the container. Mulch also helps keep roots cool in hot weather. If the rose is top-heavy when first planted, stake it for support. After the plant is established in the pot, remove the stake.

Care and Maintenance

During the growing season, roses in containers need regular watering, usually twice a week. Get in the habit of checking the soil with your index finger; water whenever the soil is dry to a depth of 1 to 2 inches. Soak the soil each time you water. Avoid splashing water on the leaves, especially if watering in the afternoon; roses that go through an entire night with wet foliage often develop leaf-spot disease. If you must water with an overhead sprinkler, do so in early morning so that the leaves dry out before nightfall.

Roses are heavy feeders, particularly selections that bloom repeatedly from spring to fall. Fertilize containerized roses at least three times a year—early in the spring, summer, and fall—by scratching a controlled-release rose fertilizer into the surface of the potting mix. When plants are flowering, feed once with rose food or balanced fertilizer in liquid form. Deadhead (cut off) spent blooms to promote repeat flowering. In the fall, after you fertilize for the last time, leave some spent blossoms on the plant. These will develop into rose hips (fruits).

In the winter, roses in containers are more subject to extremes of temperature than are roses in the ground. Potted roses may not be damaged by a light frost, but most types need protection when temperatures fall to 20 degrees. If average low temperatures are below 20 degrees in your area in the winter, you should prepare your roses for the cold. Mound straw over the plants or house them in a greenhouse or a cool basement. Water plants brought indoors sparingly to discourage growth. Do not fertilize until you take the plants outside in the spring and you see signs of new growth.

Dependable, disease-tolerant roses, such as Iceberg, are always the best choice for containers.

Prune roses in late winter or early spring, before the plants leaf out. Remove weak or diseased canes, winter-damaged wood, and any branches that cross or rub others. Some spring climbers bloom on old wood; prune these when their shows are over. The beginning of the growing season is also the time to do general pruning for shaping roses and for reducing their size if they have outgrown their container. Do this in late winter before new shoots appear.

Roses will survive for years in containers, given the proper location and care. Still, it is usually necessary to repot every three to five years. One clue that a rose needs repotting is an increase in watering frequency and a decrease in bloom size. The longer a rose has been in a container, the more water it needs; as time passes, a rose slowly becomes root bound, which makes it more difficult for water to be taken up by the plant's roots. (See pages 55 and 56 for general information on repotting.)

Roses are prone to develop black spot and powdery mildew. Choose disease-tolerant types to minimize problems. Roses also attract a variety of pests, such as spider mites. See pages 124 and 125 for information on pest control.

ROSES

NAME/TYPE	FEATURES	SEASON	NATURAL SIZE	LIGHT	WATER	RANGE	PESTS/ DISEASES	COMMENTS
Cecile Brunner (The Sweetheart Rose) Polyantha Available as a climber	19th-century classic mounding shrub with 1-inch double, light pink flowers; sweetly fragrant; few thorns; repeat bloomer	Summer to fall	3 to 4 feet tall	Full sun	Medium to high	Zones 7 to 10	Disease tolerant	Set out in early spring; protect from cold in Zone 7; prune lightly; small blooms have perfect hybrid tea form
Duchesse de Brabant Hybrid tea	Old-fashioned rose, with 2- to 3-inch double, fragrant, pink flowers; everblooming in Lower South	Spring to fall	2 to 4 feet tall	Full sun	Medium to high	Zones 8 to 10	Little or no spraying required	Set out in early spring; protect from cold in Zone 8; flowers on old wood; dislikes heavy pruning
The Fairy Polyantha	1930s rose; mounding shrub with clusters of small, light pink flowers; slightly fragrant; fernlike foliage, comes in red; profuse bloomer	Spring to fall	2 to 4 feet tall	Full sun	Medium to high	Zones 7 to 10	Disease tolerant	Set out in early spring; protect from cold in Zone 7; deadhead to promote blooming; tends to bloom after rain
French Lace Floribunda	Bushy rose with 3 to 4 double flowers in clusters of 1 to 8; ivory white flowers; carnation-scented; everblooming	Spring to fall	2½ to 3 feet tall	Full sun	Medium to high	Zones 7 to 10	Aphids, spider mites (good disease-tolerance)	Set out in early spring; protect in winter in Zone 7; feed and water regularly; displays attractive foliage
Maman Cochet Hybrid tea	Old-fashioned rose with 3- to 4-inch double, creamy rose-pink flowers; fragrant; everblooming in Lower South	Spring to fall	2½ to 4 feet tall	Full sun	Medium to high	Zones 8 to 10	Aphids, spider mites	Set out in early spring; protect from cold in Zone 8; flowers on old wood; dislikes heavy pruning
Minnie Pearl Miniature	Upright shrub with double, light pink-coral flowers with hybrid tea shape; slightly fragrant; blooms constantly	Spring to fall	1 to 1½ feet tall	Full sun	Medium to high	Zones 6 to 10	Powdery mildew, spider mites	Set out in early spring; protect in winter in Zone 6; water and feed regularly; vigorous grower
Snow Bride Miniature	Upright shrub with 1-inch single, white flowers with hybrid tea buds; flowers in large clusters; easy to grow; everblooming	Spring to fall	1 to 1½ feet tall	Full sun	Medium to high	Zones 6 to 10	Powdery mildew, spider mites	Set out in early spring; protect from winter cold in Zone 6; water and feed regularly
Starina Miniature	Upright shrub with scarlet-orange, hybrid tea-shaped blooms; good cut flower; vigorous grower; everblooming	Spring to fall	15 to 18 inches tall	Full sun	Medium to high	Zones 6 to 10	Powdery mildew, spider mites	Set out in early spring; protect in winter in Zone 6; water and feed regularly; highly rated by American Rose Society
Sun Flare Floribunda	Bushy rose with clusters of 3-inch semidouble, lemon yellow flowers; mild licorice fragrance; everblooming	Spring to fall	2 to 3 feet tall	Full sun	Medium to high	Zones 7 to 10	Aphids, spider mites (disease tolerant)	Set out in early spring; protect in winter in Zone 7; feed and water regularly; displays glossy, deep green foliage

Tropicals

Bougainvillea blooms from May to October in the confines of a pot.

Many tropicals are ideal for summer shows in pots. Most are medium-sized to large specimen plants with striking flowers, foliage, form, or fragrance, or some combination of these. They are worth the extra effort it takes to coax them through the winter, because they become more impressive with each passing year.

Growing Tropicals in Containers

Tropical plants include a vast group of exotics, each with its own special charm. For summer color, choose angel's trumpet, bougainvillea, hibiscus, or lantana; these bloom with abandon. Use banana plants,

When the weather turns hot in June, many plants wilt, but heat-loving tropicals are in their element.

A grouping of cacti creates a casual atmosphere in this patio garden.

Few tropicals are as showy as angel's trumpet.

elephant's ears, or flowering ginger—all rapid producers of lush emerald foliage—to create a privacy screen for a seating area or to add a tropical background for a birdbath or a garden pool. Place pots of jasmine near gathering spots so that visitors can enjoy the exotic fragrance.

Citrus and bay are elegant when trained as topiaries or single-trunked trees. Place them in pots and then position the standards on each side of the front entrance to the house or at the top of patio steps to welcome guests. Group pots of cacti, succulents, and other desert tropicals on a patio or a deck to evoke the feeling of a courtyard.

Tropicals can be used to attract garden wildlife. Hummingbirds will feed on the nectar in the flowers of tropical salvias. Or you might want to plant lantana—the pink and yellow blossoms will entice a variety of butterflies from summer to the first frost.

Although all tropicals are *tender* (not cold-hardy), they differ in their water and sunlight requirements. Note how much sunlight your chosen site receives; then select tropicals that thrive in these light conditions. (See the chart on pages 121–123 for a list of tropical plants suitable for container gardening.)

Place containerized plants where they can be watered easily, as they need frequent watering during hot weather. Put large pots on casters to make moving plants indoors simpler when cold weather arrives. If you have an extensive collection of tropicals, group them by cultural requirements, such as their need for water, to make caring for them easier.

Choosing Containers for Tropicals

Tender tropicals can be divided into three groups, based on their natural habitat: rain-forest, Mediterranean, and desert plants. Each type has different growing requirements, which influence the choice of container. With the exception of desert plants, most tropicals are medium-sized to large and must have pots deep enough to accommodate them. A pot must have a drainage hole but need not be freezeproof, since tropicals cannot be left outside in the winter anyway. Raising tropicals in containers gives you the chance to experiment with colorful Mexican or other regional pottery.

Rain-forest plants. These tropicals have lush foliage, grow quickly, and require frequent watering and fertilizing. This group includes angel's trumpet, banana plants, elephant's ears, flowering ginger, hibiscus, and night-blooming cereus. All rain-forest plants grow enough in a single season to require a large container base (at least 16 inches in diameter) for balance. Top-heavy plants need fairly sturdy containers to keep them from toppling during summer storms. Many gardeners prefer to grow rain-forest plants in plastic or resin pots, which don't dry out as quickly as clay. If you plan to be away in the summer, use a self-watering pot or a drip-irrigation system with a timer.

Mediterranean plants. Some well-known plants of this type are bay, citrus, gardenia, jasmine, lantana, and tropical salvias. They are able to tolerate short periods of drought because they have tough leathery leaves that don't lose as much moisture as the rain-forest plants. Most of these plants need six hours of full sunlight a day. They are medium-sized to large plants and require substantial containers—at least 16 inches in diameter—when fully grown. Mediterranean types grow well in clay, concrete, plastic, or resin containers.

Desert plants. This group includes cacti, palms, and succulents. Cacti and succulents are generally small plants that perform well in small to medium-sized containers, such as dish-shaped pots, strawberry jars, or concrete troughs. Palms, most cacti, and succulents grow best in pots that dry out quickly, such as those made of clay or concrete; desert plants tend to rot if kept constantly wet.

These tropicals need direct sunlight and are able to survive drought. During humid, rainy summers, make sure they don't become waterlogged. Well-drained soil is a must. Placing containers in a dry spot near the foundation or under the eaves of the house helps prevent rot as long as the location is sunny.

Small succulents are ideal for planting in porous clay pots that dry out quickly.

Sizable clay or concrete pots provide enough weight to keep banana plants or citrus trees from toppling over during storms or high winds. Place the containers on casters so that you can move the plants easily. You might decide to turn a heavy container into a cachepot; plant the tropical in a slightly smaller plastic pot and then slide it inside the heavy decorative container. Another option is to put a 1-inch layer of pebbles or coarse gravel at the bottom of a light pot and use a potting mix that contains sand to add weight. Or drive a stake into the ground behind a top-heavy potted plant and unobtrusively tie the plant to the stake. If you wish to train a potted vine to climb a trellis, attach the trellis to a stake in the ground rather than placing the trellis in the container.

Vining tropicals, such as mandevilla, need to wrap around a stake or a trellis.

117

Set out such tropicals as croton when the weather turns warm in the spring.

Planting Tropicals in Pots

Plant tropicals in late spring or in the summer—the earlier the better, as you will have more time to enjoy your plants. Containers can be heavy after they are filled with potting soil and plant material, so set your pots in place before you begin planting.

To prepare a pot, cover the drainage hole with coarse screen so that soil and roots stay inside. Then add a layer of gravel to keep the pot from tipping over in the wind. At particularly windy sites, such as balconies or rooftops, fill a third of the pot with gravel. Add moistened potting mix until the pot is about three-quarters full.

If planting a tall tropical, use a potting mix designed to anchor trees and shrubs. This medium needs to have more substance than a potting mix for smaller plants in order to ensure the stability of top-heavy plants. To make your own mix, blend equal parts of a quality peat-based potting mix with well-rotted pine bark for a moderate-weight soil to support a tall plant's trunk, even in a light wind. The rotted pine bark retains moisture longer than peat moss does; it also provides more stability and is less expensive. This slightly denser soil mix is also good to use with tropicals planted in containers in full sunlight, because it helps prevent the soil mix and the plant from drying out. At planting, mix controlled-release fertilizer into the potting soil, if it is not already included.

When planting a tropical in its new home, gently remove the plant from its original container and untangle the matted root ball. If the plant is root bound, make a cut in the bottom of the root ball and tease apart the roots. Place the tropical in the new container so that the top of the root ball is within 2 inches of the rim. Fill in around the sides of the root ball with moistened potting mix, firming the surface with your fingers. Level off the mix within $\frac{1}{2}$ to 1 inch of the rim. Do not fill the pot too full, or the soil will wash out when you water.

Low-growing pentas and petunias make great additions to pots containing tall tropicals, such as this yellow-flowering hibiscus.

Also, do not set the plant too high in the pot (a common mistake with container gardening).

After planting, water thoroughly. To create additional interest, set low-growing or trailing plants, such as verbena, around the base of the plant. Or mulch the plant with large smooth stones, shells, or pinecones to slow evaporation.

A large tropical can be top-heavy when it is first planted, requiring a supporting stake in the container. Place the stake outside the root ball but close enough to tie the stake loosely to the plant.

Care and Maintenance

Tropicals differ in their moisture requirements, but all need to be watered regularly. (See the chart on pages 121–123 for specifics on each plant.) Rain-forest types may require daily watering during hot, dry weather; Mediterranean plants often need watering only two or three times a week, and desert tropicals do well with less moisture. To simplify watering, group these plants by type in the landscape.

In general, rain-forest plants grow quickly and, therefore, require frequent fertilizing. Give them liquid fertilizer once a month, in addition to the controlled-release fertilizer incorporated into their potting soil at planting; fertilize Mediterranean types the same way. Desert plants are light feeders and do not need applications of liquid fertilizer at planting if the controlled-release granular fertilizer in the container is renewed every three to six months.

Be sure to move tender tropicals inside when temperatures fall below 40 degrees. If possible, set plants in a sunroom or in a west- or south-facing window. Keep plants several inches away from the windowpane, as cold air will penetrate the glass. If there isn't a sunny place available, overwinter plants in a frostfree but somewhat cool room, such as a basement. Water these plants sparingly so that plants go semidormant (as many tropicals do in their natural habitats). Some plants will overwinter more successfully than others. A sunny spot near a basement window is a good location as long as the plant is not touching the glass.

Before setting plants outside in the spring, when the threat of frost has passed and the weather is warm, trim back overgrown plants

Such large-leafed, lush rain-forest plants as banana plants can be brought into a cool garage basement for the winter.

and transfer potbound tropicals to larger containers. To avoid burning tender leaves, introduce plants to strong, outdoor light slowly. Place them in the shade initially; then gradually move them into stronger sunlight over a period of several weeks.

If you do not have an appropriate room in which to overwinter tropicals, consider growing them as annuals. Purchase plants at the beginning of the season, when they are small and usually inexpensive—tropicals grow fast enough to give you a great deal of pleasure during one long summer.

Tropicals, such as this calamondin orange, require less moisture indoors during the winter; if overwatered, they may rot.

TROPICALS

NAME/SPECIES & SELECTIONS	FEATURES	SEASON	NATURAL SIZE	LIGHT	WATER	RANGE	PESTS/ DISEASES	COMMENTS
Aloe *Aloe arborescens,* *A. variegata,* *A. vera*	Clumps of succulent leaves, often banded or streaked; colorful flowers; great variation in size; most are South African	Spring to fall	6 inches to 18 feet tall, 6 inches to 8 feet wide	Full sun to partial shade	Low to medium	Zone 10	None specific	Set outdoors in late spring after last frost; easy to grow; aloe vera juice used in folk medicine for burns; large species is classic plant for urn
Angel's Trumpet *Brugmansia candida,* *B. suaveolens,* *B. versicolor*	Bell-shaped flowers, 8 to 10 inches long, drape from shrub; fragrant at night; exotic blooms in white, peach, pink, red, and orange	Summer to fall	10 to 15 feet tall, 3 to 8 feet wide	Full sun to shade	Medium	Zones 8 to 10	None specific	Set out in spring after last frost; makes great specimen plant; prune back in early spring before setting plant outdoors; all parts poisonous if ingested
Banana *Musa acuminata,* *M. coccinea,* *M. paradisiaca* Dwarf Cavendish	Large leaves, up to 9 feet long; great for pools and patios; Dwarf Cavendish has edible fruit; fast grower	Summer to fall	4 to 20 feet tall, 4 to 8 feet wide	Full sun to partial shade	Medium to high	Zones 9 and 10	None specific	Set out in spring after last frost; place out of wind; fertilize well; in fall, cut off top before moving indoors; only bears fruit in Tropical South
Bay *Laurus nobilis*	Evergreen shrub or tree; leaves are a culinary favorite; aromatic with clusters of small yellow flowers; slow grower	All seasons; blooms in spring	12 to 40 feet tall, 8 to 15 feet wide	Full sun to partial shade	Medium	Zones 8 to 10	None specific	Set out in spring after last frost; can be shaped as topiary globe or cone; classic formal container plant used as accent or focal point
Bougainvillea *Bougainvillea species*	Romantic, vibrantly colored bracts; good for hanging baskets and espalier; fast grower	Spring to fall	1 to 4 feet tall, 1 to 6 feet wide; 20 feet long when trained as vine	Full sun to partial shade	Medium to high	Zones 9 and 10	None specific	Set out in spring after last frost; fragile roots, so keep root ball intact during repotting; as plant grows, supply sturdy supports and keep shoots tied up to avoid wind damage
Cacti Barrel *(Echinocactus species),* Cushion *(Mammillaria* and *Coryphantha species),* Pipe *(Cereus species)* Prickly pear *(Opuntia humifusa)*	Easy care with unusual features, such as spines, ribbed stems, and hairiness on some; tolerant of extreme heat; brightly colored flowers	Spring to fall; blooms in spring	2 inches to 80 feet tall, depending on species; most are under 1 foot tall and equally wide	Full sun	Low to medium (during flowering)	Zones 7 to 10	None specific	Some species are winter hardy; set tender ones out in spring after last frost; wear leather gloves to handle cacti safely when transplanting
Chinese Fan Palm *Livistona chinensis*	Evergreen; classic palm leaves droop at outer edges; self-cleaning; slow grower	Spring to fall	5 to 15 feet tall, 8 to 10 feet wide	Full sun	Medium	Zones 9 and 10	None specific	Set out in spring after last frost; excellent specimen or accent; great for pool areas; hardiest of this genus

TROPICALS

NAME/SPECIES & SELECTIONS	FEATURES	SEASON	NATURAL SIZE	LIGHT	WATER	RANGE	PESTS/ DISEASES	COMMENTS
Citrus *Citrus species* Calamondin, kumquat, lemon, lime, mandarin, orange	Incredibly fragrant flowers; edible, colorful fruit; glossy leaves; evergreen	Spring to fall	6 to 30 feet tall, depending on species; 6 to 15 feet wide	Full sun	High	Zones 9 and 10	Leaf miner, scale, spider mites	Set out in spring after last frost; ideal for scented gardens; water carefully, not allowing roots to dry or to stay wet
Croton *Codiaeum variegatum*	Brightly colored, large, glossy leaves; red, yellow, purple, bronze, pink, and variegated	Spring to fall	6 feet tall, 3 to 4 feet wide	Full sun to shade, depending on species	Medium to high	Zone 10	Mealybugs spider mites, thrips	Set out in spring after last frost; be careful when repotting, as leaves may cause skin irritation; handsome accent plant
Elephant's Ear *Alocasia amazonica,* *A. macrorrhiza,* *A. odora*	Lush tropical with green, black, and purple leaves resembling elephant's ear; leaves up to 2 feet long	Summer to fall	5 feet tall, 3 to 4 feet wide (each plant, not clump)	Partial shade	Medium to high	Zones 9 and 10	None specific	Set out bulb or tuber in late spring after last frost; old-fashioned favorite; protect foliage from the wind; juices are poisonous if ingested
Eucalyptus *Eucalyptus cinerea,* *E. neglecta,* *E. niphophila*	Fragrant, blue-green foliage; drought-tolerant; leaves oval or lance shaped; fast grower	Summer to fall	20 to 70 feet tall, 10 to 30 feet wide	Full sun	Low to medium	Zones 9 and 10	None specific	Set out in late spring after last frost; popular in herb gardens; often grown as annual; excellent cut foliage
Fig *Ficus species* *F. nitida,* Fiddle-leaf fig (*F. lyrata*), Rubber plant (*F. elastica*), Weeping fig (*F. benjamina*)	Glossy leaves vary greatly in shape by species; rubber plant has magnolia-like leaves, fiddleleaf fig has fiddle-shaped leaves	Spring to fall	20 to 40 feet tall, equally wide, depending on species	Full sun to light shade	Medium	Zone 10	Scale	Set out in spring after last frost; protect from wind; popular houseplants also used as outdoor container plants
Gardenia *Gardenia jasminoides* Cold-hardy selections include Chuck Hayes, Four Seasons, Klein's Hardy	Highly fragrant, silky white flowers on evergreen shrub; shiny lime green leaves	All seasons; blooms in summer	2 to 8 feet tall, 3 to 5 feet wide	Full sun to partial shade	Medium	Zones 8 to 10 (site on SSW location to protect from cold in Zone 8)	Whitefly	Set out in spring after last frost; place near door or deck where fragrance can be enjoyed; Dwarf gardenia (*G. radicans*) grows 6 to 12 inches tall, makes good companion for taller potted plants
Ginger Lily *Hedychium coccineum,* *H. coronarium,* *H. flavum,* and many others Elizabeth, Gold Flame, Pradhanii	Fragrant flowers appear on dense spikes late in the season; various shades of white, pink, and yellow flowers; handsome, exotic-looking foliage	Summer to fall	2 to 9 feet tall, 2 to 3 feet wide	Full sun to partial shade	High	Zones 8 to 10	None specific	Set out in late spring after last frost; old-fashioned favorite, popular in scented gardens; plants may require staking
Mandevilla *Mandevilla amabilis,* *M. splendens* Alice duPont (pink)	Vining plants with very showy, trumpet flowers in saturated colors ranging from white to pink to red	Spring to fall	12 to 30 feet long, when trained as vine	Full sun to partial shade	Medium	Zones 8 to 10	None specific	Set out in late spring after last frost; great patio plant or fast-growing summer vine for arbor or column

TROPICALS

NAME/SPECIES & SELECTIONS	FEATURES	SEASON	NATURAL SIZE	LIGHT	WATER	RANGE	PESTS/ DISEASES	COMMENTS
Night-blooming Cereus *Hylocereus undatus*	Type of cactus with waxy, fragrant flowers, up to 12 inches long, that appear at night; flowers live 1 night; blooms throughout summer; edible, sweet fruit	Summer	15 feet to 30 feet tall, 3 to 4 feet wide	Full sun to partial shade	Low to medium	Zone 10	None specific	Set outside in late spring after last frost; water regularly until flowering, then sparingly through summer to encourage flowering; in winter, keep air moist indoors and night temperature above 55° F
Salvia *Salvia species* Indigo Spires, Mealy-cup sage (*S. farinacea*), Mexican bush sage (*S. leucantha*), Pineapple sage (*S. elegans*)	Flowers on spikes ranging in color from white, red, and true blue to purple/white bicolored; pineapple sage has sweetly flavored, edible leaves	Summer to frost	2 to 4 feet tall, equally wide	Full sun to partial shade	Low to medium	Zones 8 to 10	None specific	Set out in spring after last frost; Mexican bush sage blooms late summer/fall; over 20 species of salvia available; like dryer locations; almost all attract hummingbirds
Scented Geranium *Pelargonium species*	Apple-, lemon-, lime-, peppermint-, and rose-scented foliage tolerates hot, humid weather; inconspicuous blooms	Spring to fall	1 to 3 feet tall, equally wide	Full sun to partial shade	Medium	Zones 9 and 10	Aphids, spider mites, whiteflies	Set out in late spring after last frost; use in baskets and window boxes; popular in herb gardens; leaves good for jellies, tea, and potpourri
Star Jasmine *Trachelospermum* Asian star jasmine (*T. asiaticum*), Confederate jasmine (*T. jasminoides*), Variegatum	Evergreen with sweetly fragrant, pinwheel blossoms, up to 1 inch in diameter; use Asian star jasmine as trailer; train Conferederate jasmine on structure as vine	Spring to fall	1½ to 2 feet tall, 4 to 5 feet wide; Confederate jasmine grows to 20 feet when trained as vine	Full sun to shade	Medium	Zones 8 to 10	None specific	Set outside in spring after last frost; Asian star jasmine flowers are creamy yellow; Confederate jasmine flowers are white, and vine needs support; both plants attract bees, good for scented gardens
Succulents *Crassula species, Echeveria, Euphorbia, Sedum* and many others	Fleshy, green-leafed plants in many different sizes, shapes, and forms; drought tolerant; flowers in summer attract bees	Spring to fall	2 inches to 3 feet tall, 1 to 3 feet wide	Full sun	Low to medium	Zones 7 to 10	None specific	Some species are frost tolerant; set out tender species in spring after last frost; ideal for sunny, western exposures and clay containers; group pots of different succulents together for impact; old-fashioned favorite
Tropical Hibiscus *Hibiscus rosa-sinensis*	Bright, saucerlike flowers, up to 8 inches in diameter; colors range from white to red, yellow to apricot/orange; blooms continuously	Spring to fall	6 to 15 feet tall, 3 to 5 feet wide	Full sun	Medium to high	Zones 9 and 10	Whitefly	Set out in late spring after last frost; fertilize every 2 weeks to promote bloom; pinching increases flower production; double forms available; attracts hummingbirds

Pest Control

Fortunately, container gardening eliminates many soilborne diseases and problems with pests. Still, plants in containers are susceptible to some of the same insects and diseases that plague permanent plantings. Timing is important to eliminate the first generations before the pests are able to reproduce and cause more damage.

INSECT	Description/Damage	Control
Aphid	Tiny, pear-shaped insects appear by hundreds on new growth and flowerbuds; stems, leaves, and flowers are distorted	Spray with strong jet of insecticidal soap and repeat frequently; spray susceptible trees and shrubs with horticultural oil in late winter to kill overwintering eggs
Beetles Blister, Colorado Potato, Cucumber, Flea, Japanese, Mexican Bean	Hard-bodied insects that chew on leaves and tender stems of plants; some beetles can defoliate vegetables or, in the case of Japanese beetles, reach such large numbers that they damage trees and shrubs	Handpick beetles and egg clusters (wear gloves) when they first appear or shake them to the ground; if plant is threatened, spray with an approved insecticide
Borers Squash Vine, Twig	Borers, the larvae of moths or beetles, tunnel through tree trunks and branches as well as the stems of vegetables like squash; plants quickly begin to wilt and show signs of distress	Trees and shrubs attacked by borers need prompt attention, so call your Extension Service agent for recommended control or get professional help; plant squash early before borers become numerous or cut off infected stem
Bugs Squash Bug, Stinkbug	Hard-bodied insects with piercing-sucking mouthparts that are used to extract plant sap; they may also feed on fruit, causing spotting or blotching	Handpick adults early (use gloves); keep plants carefully groomed of dying or dead leaves, fruit, or flowers
Caterpillars Bagworm, Cabbage looper, Cabbageworm, Hornworm, Parsleyworm, Webworm	Caterpillars are the larvae of moths and butterflies, some of which may be desirable (such as the parsleyworm that becomes the lovely black swallowtail butterfly). Some caterpillars may chew on a tree's leaves without causing damage; others may defoliate an entire plant in a short time	Handpick caterpillars (wear gloves—some sting); use a knife to cleanly cut down bagworms and destroy them; spray with approved insecticide at first sign of infestation
Lacebug	Flat insects with lacy wings, lacebugs feed on leaves, sucking sap and causing leaves to dry, curl, and fall; they deposit tiny black spots of excrement on the underside of leaves	Spray with approved insecticide; spray tree trunks with dormant oil in winter to kill any adults that overwinter in bark
Leaf miner	Tiny caterpillar miners eat through foliage, leaving blisters and serpentine trails that disfigure leaves; tomatoes can tolerate about 50% leaf damage without hurting productivity	Remove affected leaves and egg clusters and dispose of them; spray with approved systemic insecticide; parasitic wasps are natural predators
Mealybug	Soft-bodied, ¼-inch long insects covered in white, cotton-like waxy threads; suck sap from leaves and stems, causing distorted growth and yellowing	Spray plants with stiff stream of insecticidal soap to displace bugs and repeat as needed; or apply approved insecticide; parasitic wasps are natural predators
Scale	Soft- or hard-bodied insects that cling to stems and leaf undersides; appear to be stuck to plant; suck sap, causing leaves to turn yellow	Remove affected twigs and branches; if area is small, remove scales from twigs/leaves with old toothbrush and insecticidal soap or spray with approved insecticide; to prevent, spray in winter and spring with horticultural oil; lady beetles and parasitic wasps are natural predators

INSECT

INSECT	Description/Damage	Control
Spider Mite	Minute spiderlike insects feed on buds and undersides of leaves; suck plant sap and cause foliage and buds to turn brown	Spray mites with soapy water or approved insecticide; frequent overhead watering helps knock mites from foliage and hampers reproduction; spray susceptible trees and shrubs in late winter with dormant oil to kill overwintering eggs
Thrip	Tiny torpedo-shaped insects feed inside flowers; cause blooms to turn brown where they feed	Spray with insecticidal soap or approved insecticide; spray susceptible trees and shrubs in late winter with dormant oil to kill overwintering eggs; natural predators include lady beetles and lacewings
Whitefly	Adults look like tiny white moths on leaf underside; larvae resemble drops of clear wax; feeding distorts new growth	Spray with insecticidal soap and repeat as necessary; to prevent, spray with dormant oil in late winter; predators include beetles and parasitic wasps

DISEASE

DISEASE	Description/Damage	Control
Black Spot	Fungus thrives in areas of high humidity; appears on leaves and stems as black circular spots; can defoliate entire plant	Plant resistant selections; spray with approved fungicide throughout the growing season
Blight	Characterized by sudden, rapid yellowing or browning of affected areas of Chinese juniper leaves and fruit	Plant resistant selections; avoid wetting foliage with water; remove affected parts of plants as soon as problems are noticed
Blossom-End Rot	Fruit develop round, sunken brown area on bottom (the blossom end)	Plant resistant selections; keep soil evenly moist; use fertilizer that supplies calcium or add lime to the ground before planting
Chlorosis Camellia	Usually caused by iron deficiency, this systemic condition turns plant's newer leaves yellow	Treat soil with a fertilizer that contains iron or spray with liquid fertilizer that contains iron
Fungus	Fungus diseases are among most widespread in plants, as each spore under right conditions will germinate and grow	Plant resistant selections; provide good light, good air circulation, and enough moisture to keep soil damp but not soggy; spray with approved fungicide
Leaf Spot	Fungus can cause spots on leaves; may cause leaves to yellow or drop	Remove infected leaves and spray at first sign of infestation with approved fungicide
Mildew Downy, Powdery	Fungus looks like mildew; seen as growth on surface of leaves; worse in spring and fall in cool, humid conditions	Plant resistant selections; remove affected plant parts; water in early morning or use with drip irrigation to avoid wetting leaves
Rot	Overwatering or poor drainage causes roots and crowns of plants to rot	Avoid overwatering and provide good drainage; once rot begins, it is difficult to control
Rust	Fungi that attacks leaves, stems, and fruits of plants; powdery masses of spores cover undersides of leaves; yellow mottling on upper surface; leaves may turn yellow and drop	Plant resistant selections; spray at first sign of infestation with approved fungicide
Scab	Fungus growth that produces disfiguring lesions on fruit; can cause defoliation of plant	Plant resistant selections; to control, spray just before flower buds open with approved fungicide
Wilt	Disease that inhibits plant's ability to absorb water; once affected, plant will not recover as wilt spreads within plant	Plant resistant selections; prune or remove diseased plants; provide good drainage

Index

Index